BERLITZ®

NEPAL

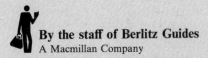

By the staff of Berlitz Guides
A Macmillan Company

How best to use this guide

- All the practical information, hints and tips that you will need before or during your trip start on page 111.

- For general background on the country and its people, turn to the sections Nepal and the Nepalis, page 6, A Brief History, page 16, and Religions of Nepal, page 24.

- All the sights to see are listed between pages 32 and 85. Our own choice of sights most highly recommended is pinpointed by the Berlitz traveller symbol.

- A special chapter devoted to trekking, how to plan and what to expect on trek, begins on page 86.

- Sports, entertainment and festivals, with a calendar of events, are described between pages 96 and 108.

- Hints on where to shop and what to buy are to be found on pages 106–107.

- Eating out possibilities are listed between pages 109 and 110.

- Finally, if there is anything you can't find instantly, refer to the index at the back of the book, pages 126 to 128.

Text: Donald Allan
Staff Editor: Christina Jackson
Layout: Max Thommen
Photography: Ashvin Gatha; p. 19 Gopal Chitrakar; p. 85 Camerapix; p. 97 courtesy of Tiger Tops Jungle Lodge; p. 99 Hans Weber; pp. 102–103 Camerapix

We would like to extend our thanks to William Ma and J.P. Singh of Gaida Wildlife Camp, Hemanta Mishra, Kishore Pandey of l'Hotel de l'Annapurna, Mr. Hada of Royal Nepal Airlines, Lisa Van Gruisen, Elizabeth Hawley, Peter and Adrienne Jackson and Dominika von Zahn for their invaluable help in the preparation of this guide.

Cartography: **Falk** Falk-Verlag, Hamburg.

Cover photo: Patan's Durbar Square; *pp. 2–3* View of Mt. Macchapuchhare from Lake Phewa.

Contents

Found an error or an omission in this Berlitz Guide? Or a change or new feature we should know about? Our editor would be happy to hear from you, and a postcard would do. Be sure to include your name and address, since in appreciation for a useful suggestion, we'd like to send you a free travel guide.

Although we make every effort to ensure the accuracy of all the information in this book, changes occur incessantly. We cannot therefore take responsibility for facts, prices, addresses and circumstances in general that are constantly subject to alteration.

Nepal and the Nepalis

Nepal reveals its surprises in layers, in waves of powerful and contrasting sensations, from dense lowland jungles to the golden treasury of medieval Kathmandu and upwards into the dazzling heights of the Himalayas—all in a space smaller than Florida. To the impact of these exotic images is added the excitement of discovery in a country long forbidden to foreigners, where the majority of the population still lives in villages days of walking from the nearest road.

Nepal is a frontier. It is the collision point where 60 million years ago the drifting continent of India drove into Asia, slowly forcing up the earth's crust to form the world's highest and still-grow-

ing mountains. It is the biological border where the flora and fauna of the tropics overlap with species of the temperate zone, producing a wealth of wildlife. It is the meeting and artistic merging point of two great religions, Hinduism and Buddhism, and of many diverse peoples, whose colourful costumes and festivals create perpetual theatre in the streets of Kathmandu. Mount Everest and more than a thousand cloud-piercing peaks are the ultimate test of human endurance for mountaineers. And Nepal is a frontier of tourism, too, off the beaten track, yet amply supplied today with facilities that cushion adventure with comfort.

Once a lake, now a verdant rice bowl, Kathmandu's valley is a treasury where golden gods bid visitors "Namaste", a welcome.

You'll probably cross the real frontier by air, at the same time getting your first thrilling view of the Himalayas. They take over the horizon, a thousand-mile reef of rock, snow and ice from Kashmir to Sikkim, and Nepal's sector of the mountain wall is the highest. Which peak is Everest? It is difficult to identify the mountains at first, even with a map. Later, you'll come to recognize their distinctive features.

Flying into Nepal you'll be struck by the green and gold of the jungles and rice paddies of the lowlands called the Terai, Nepal's breadbasket. The Terai is veined with rivers flowing towards the Ganges out of deep gorges in a range of brown mountains, heaped high like rumpled bedclothes. This is the Mahabharat Lekh, a formidable barrier running parallel to the Himalayas and rising abruptly to some 9,000 feet (nearly 3,000 m.). The Mahabharat long served to discourage invaders and even now is crossed by road only at four points. As you descend, you'll note that the contours of these steep slopes are evenly ridged by cultivated terraces. And you'll see clusters of houses and the trails that connect the communities.

8 Crossing low over this range, your aircraft will angle into the bowl of the Kathmandu Valley, encircled by hills and with the eternal snows of Ganesh Himal and Langtang soaring in the background. Tibet is only about 50 air miles (80 km.) away, but much of this distance is still traversed by caravans of yaks and donkeys that take a month to cross the high mountain passes, exchanging Nepali rice and goods for Tibetan salt as they have for countless centuries. The incongruities and anachronisms, as of jumbo jets parked beside fields where women are threshing rice by hand, will be one of your lasting impressions of Nepal.

Squeezed between two giants, India and China, Nepal is sensitive about its borders and walks a political tightrope. His Royal Highness King Birendra Bir Bikram Shah Dev, who ascended the throne in 1972, on the death of his father King Mahendra, has declared his country a "Zone of Peace". As a result, Nepal, one of the poorest countries in the world by U.N.

Restaurant cooks shop early while farm wives shiver in the capital's wholesale market.

criteria, is also one of the most aided per capita by donors of every political orientation.

Most of King Birendra's 18 million subjects are subsistence farmers growing rice, maize (corn), wheat and oilseeds. The rhythm of planting and harvesting and much else in Nepali life is governed by the monsoon rains that sweep up from the Bay of Bengal from June through September. Most of the rainfall is caught by the foothills, and not much falls as snow in the Himalayas. The mountains make one imagine Nepal to be a cold country. In fact, it is on the same latitude as southern Morocco, and Kathmandu enjoys an agreeably mild climate most of the year. The snow line starts around 16,000 feet (4,800 m.), too high for ski resorts.

Nepalis are a complex mixture of Indo-Europeans originating in the Caucasus, Dravidians from southern India, and Mongolian groups and Burmese from central and south-eastern Asia. These broad groupings are reflected around the country in the quite different features, dialects, costumes and customs of peoples from some 35 ethnic groups. Nepali, the official language, is based on Sanskrit and is a close relative of the Hindi spoken in India.

Officially, 90 per cent of Nepalis are Hindus, but Buddhism is deeply rooted in the country. The Buddha was born in the 6th century B.C. in the Terai at Lumbini. Some of the most impressive works of art and architecture around Kathmandu are Buddhist-inspired. Nepalis have achieved a harmonious co-existence of the two religions in their daily lives and happily celebrate the frequent festivals of both.

A typical planeload of tourists disembarking at Tribhuvan International Airport is broadly divisible into two groups: well-dressed Westerners, some guided by a tour leader, and backpack-toting young men and women in trekking gear. Their paths will separate on leaving the airport and will only converge from time to time at the main monuments, parks and trekking routes. In Kathmandu, the first group will take taxis to hotels with swimming pools and air-conditioning and international restaurants; the second will ride a bus to the Thamel district and one of the many simple guest houses offering lodging for as little as $2 a night. The first group will be escorted to the great temples and festivals by linguist guides, will fly to the deluxe jungle camps of the Royal Chitwan National Park and trek with a team of guide, cooks and porters; the second will hike or bike to the shrines, bus or ride a raft on white-water rivers to the jungle and carry their own gear on trek, sleeping and eating in village houses.

Both groups will have the time of their lives, and both will justifiably exult that the cost of the experience was a bargain, though their bills will differ by several decimal points. Tourism has become Nepal's biggest industry, and there is something for every budget, as well as the same glorious scenery and exotic cityscapes for every camera.

The young trekkers of the 1980s are not to be confused with the hippies of the 1960s. Drug-seekers have gone since the sale of narcotics was banned in 1973. Nor will they be mistaken for the serious mountaineers, whose expeditions are often backed up by tons of equipment, film crews and helicopters. Each year, several attempts are made on some of the great peaks—the Annapurna and Everest massifs, Manaslu, Makalu, Kanchenjunga, Cho Oyu and Dhaulagiri, all over 26,000 feet (8,000 m.)—and on several of the hundreds of still-unclimbed summits. Over a hundred of the highest are cleared by the government for climbing, and the number is steadily expanding as more and more of the back country is opened to foreigners.

The bargain-hunters who elect to "take in" Nepal only as a three-day bonus tacked on to a trip to India are making a mistake. Nepal is a country to explore and savour, not to skim. Long isolation behind the natural barriers imposed by warrior despots allowed Nepal to evolve a character all its own. Amazingly, this continued right up to the mid-20th century, when foreigners were finally permitted to enter the forbidden kingdom and found it a "living museum".

In this time-capsule they found that ancient art forms and curious customs were still vigorous. The machine had not replaced the craftsman's hand. To travel meant to go on foot for days or weeks, relying on the hospitality of villagers for food and lodging. Nature ruled man's comings and goings and spoke to him from holy places on mountains wrapped in clouds, in **11** springs, rocks and forests, and through the many voices of the gods who could protect or punish.

This is Nepal still. The arrival in the past few decades of jet aircraft and air-conditioned hotels, soda pop and vaccines hasn't changed things as much as you might expect. You can fly to the starting point of your trek, but you'll begin walking from the airstrip and within minutes you'll step back centuries. You can lie in a jungle tent and hear a tiger roar and in the morning find his pug marks in the trail around your camp. You can see a dozen different butterflies and scores of birds in half an hour, bargain for Tibetan jewellery and carpets, wander in the dusty confusion of a Kathmandu market, hear the fog-horn groan of ten-foot Tibetan trumpets, watch the blood offerings at Hindu temples, shoot world-class white-water rapids on wild rivers, ride a bike or an elephant or fly just over the tops of the highest mountains in the world. You'll see views you'll never forget and bring back great photos to prove it was all real.

Pagoda-roofed temples, golden gateways and gilded images of gods and kings, pregnant mounds of *stupas* surmounted by the all-seeing eyes of Buddha, teeming street markets and narrow alleys where artisans sell their handicrafts from holes in the wall as they have from time immemorial, the chaotic traffic mix of cabs and cows, rickshaws and bicycles, and perhaps a chariot of a deity on display—these are the uniquely Nepalese images that create the spectacle of Kathmandu and its sister cities, Patan and Bhadgaon, as well as dozens of more intimate versions in the villages of the valley.

Beyond the treasures of the valley lie the trails leading into the hills and mountains which are home to the Sherpas, Gurungs and other tribal peoples. Many have never seen a car, electric light, cinema or TV or, it might be added, a flush toilet. Trekkers get to know this side of Nepali life and hospitality at close hand. And those who walk through forests of rhododendrons, cross deep river gorges on swaying suspension bridges and climb up into the heights discover where the gods live.

Foot-powered sewing machine is high tech for a tailor whose work-shop is the street.

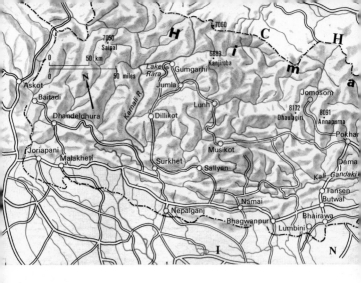

Nepal at a Glance

Geography   Nepal lies landlocked between the Tibetan Autonomous Region of China to the north and India to the south, east and west. It covers an area of 56,827 sq. mi. (147,181 sq. km.), stretches 553 mi. (885 km.) from east to west and averages 100 mi. (160 km.) from north to south. Some 25% is over 10,000 ft. (3,000 m.); 20% under 1,000 ft. (300 m.). Highest point: Mount Everest 29,028 ft. (8,848 m.). The three major rivers are the Sun Kosi, Kali Gandaki and Karnali.

Population   Estimated in 1988 at over 18 million, with about 45% under age 15. Population is growing at 2.66% annually.

Capital   Kathmandu, pop. about 500,000.

Economy   Nepal is the fourth poorest country by U.N. criteria. About two-thirds of government development expenditures are financed by foreign aid and loans. Tourism is now the biggest earner of foreign exchange. Over 94%

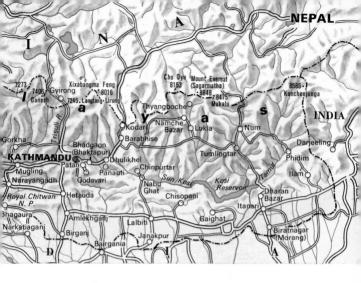

of the nation's energy is supplied by firewood, agricultural waste and animal dung. Some 94% of the population are farmers; 18% of the total area is under cultivation, with rice taking 63% of farmland to produce 2.8 million tons in 1986.

Government   Nepal is a constitutional monarchy. There are no political parties. The government operates on a four-tier system of *panchayats* (local councils), beginning at village level and rising to the Rashtriya Panchayat or National Assembly, which consists of 112 elected and 28 royally appointed members, serving a five-year term.

Language   The official language, Nepali, written in the Devanagari script, is derived from Sanskrit sources and is similar to Hindi. Some 33 other languages and dialects are spoken by 35 different tribal groups.

Religion   Hinduism claims 90% of the population. But as Hinduism and Buddhism overlap in Nepal, the figure is probably closer to 80% Hindu, 18% Buddhist and the rest Muslim.   **15**

A Brief History

Long ago, Nepalis tell, the Kathmandu Valley was a lake, the realm of snake gods, the Nagas. Then Manjushri, a wise teacher of the great god Shiva, slashed the earth with his sword, creating the slit of the Chobar Gorge and releasing the waters. All the snakes left except the King of the Nagas, who still lives in a pond that is never drained.

Geologists agree that water did once cover the valley. They suggest that an earthquake created the gorge where the Bagmati River now flows. And it is true that there are no snakes.

The early history of Nepal is thus a mixture of fact and myth, with religious lore associated with virtually every landmark and event. Initially a collection of small feuding principalities both isolated and protected by the mountainous geography, Nepal has never been a colony. From time to time, some of the feudal domains were brought together by one powerful figure, but present-day Nepal has been a unified nation for just over 200 years. The name Nepal was originally applied to the Kathmandu Valley only, and the country's formal history chiefly concerns this centre.

Unity and Fragmentation

The Licchavi dynasty of high-caste Hindu origin ruled in the valley from about A.D. 330 to 700. King Manadeva I (462–505) shook off the domination of the India Gupta emperors and extended his kingdom from the Kosi River in the east to the Gandaki River in the west and from the Terai to the Himalayan passes. A great king of this line was Amsuvarna (609–621), who married his daughter Bhrikuti to the ruler of Tibet, Srongtsen Gampo. In 640, Bhrikuti and her Chinese co-wife converted Srongtsen Gampo to Buddhism. Bhrikuti is venerated as the "Green Tara" and the Chinese wife as the "White Tara". Their images are prominent in Nepalese Buddhist art. Commercial and cultural links with Tibet, and through Tibet with China, were strengthened at this time.

More reliable records come with the next major dynasty, the Malla, which was established in about 1200 by the strongman Ari Malla. The

Malla came to Nepal in the first of several waves of Hindu fugitives from the Muslim invasion of northern India in the 11th century. Many of the refugees were nobles of the Chetri warrior caste from Rajasthan who were able to forge new feudal states in Nepal and were responsible for reinforcing Hinduism at the expense of Buddhism. The Kathmandu Valley itself was raided in 1336 by the Muslim Sultan of Bengal. In seven days he destroyed both Hindu and Buddhist temples and statues, including Swayambhunath and Pashupatinath. These great shrines were later rebuilt and expanded into their present magnificence.

Nepal and the Mallas became fragmented upon the death in 1482 of King Yaksha Malla, who divided his lands amongst his heirs. For the next three centuries Nepal had three city-states side by side in the valley—Kantipur, Lalitpur and Bhaktapur, with their hinterlands. These cities are now known as Kathmandu, Patan and Bhadgaon, though the last two are still just as often called by their old names. The Malla period saw completion of Nepal's most important palaces, temples and works of art.

Unification

Modern Nepalese history really begins with the arrival of a dynamic leader bent on unifying the country. Prithvi Narayan Shah, "The Great", was born in 1723, in the ninth generation of a line of Hindu princes of Gorkha, a hill town whose lands adjoined those of Kathmandu to the west. Like the Malla, the Shah princes had fled to Nepal from Rajasthan, rather than convert to Islam.

Prithvi Narayan Shah captured Kathmandu and Patan in 1768 and Bhadgaon a year later. Before his death in 1775, he had brought under one rule all the territory from the Mahakali River in the west to Sikkim and Darjeeling in the east. During the reign of his son, under a regent, the borders were pushed further north and west, provoking reactions from the Tibetans and Chinese as well as the British East India Company, the power to the south.

The British invaded Nepal from India in 1814 but were repulsed by the king's soldiers from Gorkha—thus earning all subsequent Nepali fighting men the name "Gurkhas" (see p. 76). The British were more successful on a second attempt in 1816, forcing Nepal **17** to give up Sikkim, Darjeeling and some territory to the far west. The peace treaty signed at Segauli established Nepal's borders pretty much as they are today. It also allowed a British representative to set up in Kathmandu, the first Western envoy to the country and, for the next century, the only one.

Rise of the Ranas

In 1846, in the course of an unsavoury palace intrigue involving an unsolved murder, meddling by the queen and the massacre of some 100 high-ranking court figures who had been lured to a palace courtyard, the instigator of these events became the power behind the throne. He was an ambitious and unscrupulous 29-year-old named Jung Bahadur Rana. Before long he had exiled the king, replaced him with the youthful crown prince and arranged to have himself and the Rana family made hereditary prime ministers.

The Ranas were the real rulers of Nepal for 104 years. The Shah kings remained, but had only ceremonial power. The Ranas kept the country in complete isolation from the outside world; foreigners weren't allowed in and few Nepalis could go out. Calling themselves Maharajahs, the prime ministers and their relatives built dozens of palaces in Kathmandu, usually in an incongruous neoclassical style. The huge white Singha Durbar palace of the prime minister had 1,700 rooms, far more than the king's. Reconstructed after a fire in 1973, it serves today as the government secretariat and meeting place of parliament.

The Ranas also brought a few modern improvements, such as water and power works for the capital, a 29-mile (50-km.) narrow-gauge railway in the Terai, a hospital and museum. There were not many motorable roads, however, and the Rolls-Royces of the Ranas were brought to Kathmandu in pieces, either on frames carried by big teams of porters or on the ropeway, a lift that still carries freight from Hetauda in the Terai over the Mahabharat range. Outside the valley, Nepal slumbered on in the Middle Ages.

Modern Times

When India became independent in 1947, pressure for change mounted within Nepal. In 1950, King Tribhuvan pretended he was going on a

King Birendra Shah Dev attended Oxford and Harvard before his coronation in 1975. Many of his Hindu subjects regard him as an incarnation of the god Vishnu.

shooting picnic and managed to escape to India. An uprising spread against the Ranas, and Prime Minister Mohan Shumshere Rana resigned in 1951. King Tribhuvan returned, a first constitution for the monarchy was installed and some foreigners were allowed into Nepal. Two years **19** later, Mount Everest was conquered.

King Mahendra acceded to the throne on the death of his father in 1955. After an experiment with elections and parliamentary democracy, King Mahendra abolished the constitution in 1962 and instituted the present system of *"panchayat* democracy". Road-building and airport construction progressed during his reign.

After King Birendra became sovereign in 1972—tenth in the line of Shah rulers since King Prithvi the Great—a referendum in which all Nepalis over 21 were eligible to vote confirmed the popular preference for the *panchayat* system over a return to multi-party democracy. But the king deferred to demands expressed in student demonstrations by making the majority of the legislature directly elected, with the council of ministers responsible to the parliament as well as to the king.

In recent years the government and foreign donors have made great efforts to develop Nepal's rather sparse natural resources. A number of hydro-electric dams are being built, roads are being extended, schools and health posts are multiplying. Progress is

offset by steep increases in the population, which stands to double every 26 years at present rates.

At the same time, almost total dependency on firewood for fuel has deforested the heavily populated middle mountain ranges and led to erosion, landslides and loss of soil for agriculture in the hills. Without trees to hold moisture, monsoon rains run off rapidly, swelling the rivers and causing severe floods downstream in India and Bangladesh. These are problems studied by the South Asian Association for Regional Cooperation (SAARC), an inter-governmental body that has its secretariat in Kathmandu.

Tourism is now the most important source of foreign exchange in Nepal. It has grown from a few thousand adventurous souls 30 years ago to a quarter of a million visitors a year, and it provides income for Nepalis in mountain villages as well as for those in urban hotels and construction jobs. The influx of foreigners has added to pressures on the Himalayan environment, but it hasn't spoiled the friendliness of Nepalis, surely among the most welcoming people on earth.

Historical Landmarks

Prehistory	The collision of the continents of India and Asia creates the Himalayas some 60 million years ago.
	Different Aryan peoples settle in the fertile Kathmandu Valley around 2,000 years ago.
6th c B.C.	Birth of Buddha at Lumbini.
330–700 A.D.	Licchavi Dynasty rules in Kathmandu Valley. Commercial and cultural links with China and Tibet are established.
11th c	First waves of Hindu refugees arrive in Nepal in the wake of the Muslim conquest of northern India.
1200	Malla Dynasty of Hindu princes from Rajasthan is founded by Ari Malla.
1336	Muslim Sultan of Bengal raids the valley, destroying temples and statues.
1482	King Yaksha Malla divides his kingdom amongst his heirs. Kathmandu, Patan and Bhadgaon are separate states.
1768	King Prithvi Narayan Shah captures Kathmandu and Patan.
1769	With the fall of Bhadgaon, Nepal becomes a unified country.
1814–1816	Hostilities with the British East India Company culminate in the Treaty of Segauli.
1846	Jung Bahadur Rana usurps royal power, establishes a line of hereditary prime ministers who keep Nepal in total isolation from the rest of the world.
1950	As opposition to Rana rule grows, King Tribhuvan escapes to India.
1951	Prime Minister Mohan Shumshere Rana resigns and King Tribhuvan returns. Nepal reopens its doors to foreigners.
1953	First ascent of Mount Everest.
1955	King Mahendra acceeds to the throne.
1962	King abolishes constitution and institutes *panchayat* democracy.
1972	King Birendra becomes sovereign and declares Nepal a "Zone of Peace".

What is a Nepali?

Nepal's 35 tribes weave a colourful ethnic tapestry. Despite their different customs and origins, all these peoples have long lived together peaceably and have created a rich national culture. Here are some of the main groups:

The **Newars**, of mixed Caucasian and Mongoloid stock, are considered to be among the earliest inhabitants of central Nepal. In medieval times, they created a highly developed urban civilization in the Kathmandu Valley, where they still predominate. Their communities of two-storey brick houses set close together are easily recognizable. Skilled Newar craftsmen can be credited with much of Nepali art and architecture.

The **Tharus** of the lowlands, a large tribe of farmers and cattlebreeders, may have been the first to migrate to Nepal from India. The **Tamangs** of the Mahabharat hill farms are Mongoloid in appearance and wear conspicuous, nose and ear jewellery. In the central mountains beyond Kathmandu live the **Gurungs** and **Magars** who, with the **Rai** and **Limbu** farther to the east, fill the ranks of Gurkha mercenaries. They are all of Mongoloid origin and tend to be Buddhists or animists. The **Thakali** who live along the route to Tibet in the Kali Gandaki Valley are famed as traders and businessmen.

In the high mountains, the **Sherpas**, of Tibetan origin, have earned the name "Tigers of the Snows" for their role in climbing expeditions. Other mountain people are collectively called **Bhotia** and include the Dolpo, Lopa and Manang.

Not tribes, but close-knit groups of Indo-Caucasian origin arising from the Hindu caste system, are the **Brahmins** and **Chetris**. Brahmins are hereditary priests, while Chetris constitute the warrior class who have always been the administrators. These groups are found all over Nepal and in all sorts of occupations, rich and poor. The royal family are Chetris, but so are many subsistence farmers in the mountains.

Tartan-draped Gurkhas earned a reputation for courage in centuries of service for Britain; Nepali faces and costumes reflect mix of Asiatic and Caucasian origins among the country's dozens of diverse tribes.

Religions of Nepal

To understand what you'll see people doing, their reactions, their festivals and works of art and architecture, you'll need to know the basics of the chief religions, Hinduism and Buddhism. The two coexist harmoniously in a fusion of faith that is unique to this country.

In Nepal, both Hindu and Buddhist temples may take the pagoda form, but all the Indian-style stone *shikara* tower temples are Hindu and all the white dome-like *stupas* are Buddhist. So are the small trail-side shrines in the high mountains called *chortens*, often surrounded by stones carved with the *Om mani padme hum* incantation—"Hail, jewel in the flower of the lotus". Small stupas found around Buddhist and Hindu temples are known as *chaityas,* erected to hold relics or in memory of individuals.

One must always walk clockwise round any temple or shrine and rotate prayer wheels in this direction.

Hinduism

Hinduism is a guide to a virtuous life and a structure for social relationships rather than a formal "church". It originated nearly 4,000 years ago with Aryan peoples who migrated to India from the vicinity of present-day Iran. These peoples revered the forces of nature personified by innumerable gods and goddesses whose activities and moral guidelines are chronicled in prayers, hymns and poetic sacred epics of great antiquity.

At the heart of Hinduism is belief in a life essence and a common soul, *atman*, in which all living things share, and in reincarnation, the soul's rebirth after death in another form. What the next form will be depends on the sum total of a person's actions in his previous life, his *karma*. Following rituals such as purifying baths, making offerings to the gods and honouring them in festivals will lead to reincarnation in a higher form. The highest is liberation from the nuisance of repeated rebirth in this imperfect world.

Most Hindu temples in Nepal are dedicated to the great gods Vishnu and Shiva or their consorts and offspring.

A domestic Shiva and Parvati take in Durbar Square scene.

Over the doorway is a semi-circular panel called a *torana* with images of the resident god to help you identify who's who.

Vishnu is the preserver of life; Shiva is the destroyer whose destruction makes new beginnings possible. The third member of the Hindu "trinity" is Brahma, whose only task was to create the world. All this would be simple enough but for the fact that the gods have appeared on earth in different incarnations, or *avatars*, with different names, forms and natures. Some even assimilate Buddhist and primitive non-Hindu local deities. If you are confused, join the club—so are the experts.

Vishnu, for example, can be Narayan, floating on the primeval ocean or lying on a bed of snakes. He is also Rama, the model prince and star of the *Ramayana* epic, and Krishna, a lusty hero who is the central figure of the *Bhagavad Gita*, a section of the *Mahabharata* epic. Vishnu is shown with four arms, holding a lotus, a club, a conch shell and a disk, often seated on a snake, symbolizing eternity. Vishnu may appear in art as a fish, a tortoise, a boar, a man-lion or a dwarf, the first five of his nine *avatars*. The ninth, according to some Hindus, was the Buddha. His tenth incarnation, to rescue the world from evil by destroying it and beginning a new cycle, is due about 540,000 years from now. Rama carries a bow and arrows. Krishna may have a blue face, an after-effect of swallowing a poison that threatened the world. He is often represented playing a flute or sporting with the milkmaids he seduced.

Shiva, as Pashupati, is the guardian of Nepal. He has 1,008 names in Sanskrit literature. As Mahadev, he is lord of reproduction represented by the *lingam*, a phallus symbol often appearing in his temples as a stump of stone rising from the female symbol, a disk called the *yoni*. Shiva is also lord of learning and dance. As bloodthirsty Bhairav, he destroys at will. But he also destroys ignorance and misfortunes—the reason he is the symbol of Royal Nepal Airlines! Shiva generally has a frightening aspect, fanged and festooned with skulls. A

Sadhus, Hindu holy mendicants, are a common sight around religious shrines.

statue of Nandi, the bull, and the trident sign mark the temples of Shiva.

The wives of these gods also have numerous names and attributes. Lakshmi, Vishnu's wife, was created from ocean foam, like Venus, and is goddess of good fortune and beauty. Shiva's wife is Parvati, also called Annapurna in Nepal. She, too, has various aspects. As Kali, she is horrible to look at, with a long tongue and staring eyes, and is kept satisfied by the blood of sacrificed animals. As Durga, she is fierce, riding a tiger and brandishing a sword. Parvati has more benevolent aspects, such as Taleju, patron deity of the Nepali royal family, and Devi. Shiva and Parvati are the parents of the elephant-headed Ganesh, easily the most popular of the family because he is capable of assuring the success or failure of any venture.

Two other often-represented deities are Hanuman, the monkey god and helper of Rama, and Garuda, the winged birdman who carries Vishnu. He regularly appears kneeling before temples to his master, his palms joined together in the traditional *namaste* gesture of greeting and homage.

Most Nepalis begin the day by making an offering to a god or goddess whose favour they seek. This act, called *puja*, may consist of placing a small dish of oil, grains of rice or flower petals at an altar in the home, at a temple or a tree, stone or other place sacred to the spirits. A priest or respected family member may place a *tika*, a dot of red paste on a worshipper's forehead, the spot where the beam of enlightenment is thought to emanate.

Buddhism

Siddhartha Gautama was born a prince in the line of Sakya kings in the 6th century B.C. near present-day Lumbini. As a young man he was sheltered from the harsh realities of life, until one day he saw a sick man, then an aged blind man and finally a body being carried to burial. Profoundly shaken, he left his wife and small son and became a wandering beggar, searching for the meaning of existence. But the life of an ascetic and the wisdom of Hindu teachers still did not satisfy his quest. Finally, seated in meditation beneath a pipal tree at Bodh Gaya in India, the "Four Noble Truths" were revealed to him.

Whirling prayers inside wheels multiplies Sherpa's devotions.

He became the Buddha, the Enlightened One, and embarked on travels to spread his beliefs.

Buddha never claimed to be divine and in fact emphasized that all men could by their own efforts follow his path to enlightenment and the blissful state of *nirvana*, release from the cycle of repeated births and deaths. His "Four Noble Truths" are: all life is suffering; suffering is caused by desires; desires can be suppressed; and the way to be- **29** come free of desires is to follow eight "right" principles—the Eightfold Path. These are right views, right intentions, right speech, right conduct, right livelihood, right effort, right mindfulness and right contemplation.

After the Buddha's death at the age of 80, Buddhism eventually split into two main lines, those who strictly followed his teachings, the Theravada or Hinayana school of Sri Lanka and South-east Asia, and those who allowed new interpretations, the Mahayana Buddhists of China, Japan, Korea, Tibet, India and Nepal.

The Mahayana allowed worship of the Buddha and recognized other holy figures. These include a number of other Buddhas, to be approached for favour through meditation, and saint-like Bodhisattvas who achieved enlightenment but remained active to help humankind find the right path. In Nepal, Bodhisattvas often seem to blend with Hindu gods and resemble them. The Bodhisattvas Lokesvara, Manjushri and Machendra are especially popular in the Kathmandu Valley with both religions.

Buddhism in Tibet and Nepal is strongly influenced by

Buddhist pilgrims gain extra merit by climbing the steep steps to Swayambhunath.

elements of Tantrism, techniques to speed up enlightenment. These include learning physical and mental control

through yoga exercises, and prayer and meditation rituals such as repeating certain phrases, or *mantras*, and concentrating on geometrical designs called *mandalas*. Prayer wheels and flags multiply the power of prayer by adding to devotion the energy of movement. Inside each prayer wheel is a scroll covered with prayers. Tantrism is also the source of the male and female symbols of the *vajra* thunderbolt (also called *dorje*) and the bell (*ghanta*), usually present in Buddhist ceremonies, and of the system of *lamas* or high priests, who are held to be reincarnations of holy men. **31**

Where to Go

In planning your trip to Nepal, you can divide your time between several quite different itineraries, according to your interests.

Kathmandu and the landmarks of its neighbouring towns and valley shrines are the prizes that attract most visitors to Nepal. There is nothing quite like them on earth, a fact recognized by Unesco in declaring the complex a cultural World Heritage Site to be cherished and protected for all mankind.

Although they are so close to Kathmandu as almost to be suburbs, the sister cities of Patan and Bhadgaon each have a distinct character and unique attractions. For 300 years they were separate kingdoms with related, but not always friendly, Malla rulers until forcibly united in the late 18th century.

Within and beyond the valley are many more sights worth taking in on day trips, including viewpoints on the valley's rim from where you can see the Himalayas at sunrise and sunset, particularly recommended if you are not planning to extend your stay with a trek.

Jungle visitors to the Royal Chitwan National Park may choose to rough it or enjoy royal comforts. Either way, the pleasures of the park can be appreciated, but you may determine your site by whether you want to see tigers or rhinos or bird-watch.

For some, trekking will be the main purpose of a trip to Nepal. The special section on trekking gives hints and tips on what to expect, what to take along, the dangers to avoid and a brief description of the more popular treks (see pp. 86–95).

Reservations for hotels, jungle lodges, flights to and within Nepal can be hard to confirm in the busiest seasons if you wait too long. Planning is important, but so is flexibility. One should allow a few extra days for contingencies, perhaps a flight cancelled by weather in the mountains or just your on-the-spot realization that there's more to do and see than you expected.

The question where to begin is easy: exotic Kathmandu, capital and gateway to Nepal.

Three generations take a break outside sturdy Newar farm home.

Kathmandu

The sights, sounds and smells of Old Kathmandu bombard the senses. The centre of the capital is a kaleidoscope of golden rooftops, multicoloured costumes, steep temple steps layered with wares like market shelves, country women hawking produce spread on the streets, sari-draped matrons placing flower petals on altars to grimacing gods, the sudden eruption of a band of musicians or a troop of goats across your path, the scent of marigold garlands and of dumplings fried in oil, the

constant jangling of bicycle bells and rickshaw horns. It's all too much to take in at once.

Begin with an organized tour of the city or engage a guide through a travel agency. Sort out the main features and then return on your own for a closer, calmer look. Few streets are signposted, so with the help of a good map orient yourself by a few major landmarks. Finding hidden gems is one of the great rewards of

In clear winter air, Himalayas seem very close to Kathmandu.

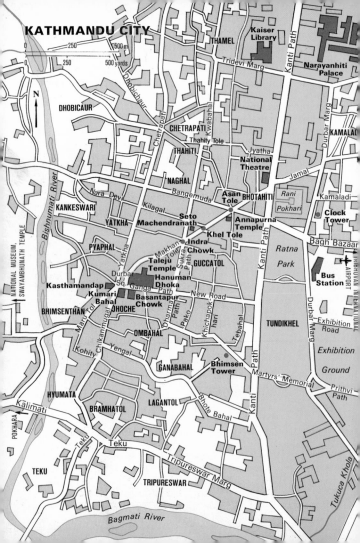

exploring Kathmandu on foot, by bicycle or rickshaw. There are no helpful signs to guide you, and organized tours rarely penetrate these corners. Assuming a minimum of stops for shopping, the following walking tour will take a very full half day.

A good place to start is the square basin of water with a small white temple to Shiva in the middle known as the **Rani Pokhari** (Queen's Pond). It lies at the northern end of the large open space that divides the old city from the newer districts. This space includes the Ratna Park and Tundikhel parade ground. To the south of the open space is the Bhimsen Tower, a useful landmark. Directly across the street from the corner of the Rani Pokhari where the *tempos*—motorized rickshaws—start is the National Theatre.

Walking south from the Rani Pokhari, you'll pass a huge **market** in an open field, where crowds of Nepalis are shopping for clothes and household goods. Off to one side, goats or ducks and chickens in bamboo baskets are sold for sacrifice on festival days (and later eaten). The avenue alongside is **Kanti Path** (King's Way), lined with former palaces of the Rana family now used for public buildings.

Cross Kanti Path where a portal leads into the busy shopping street nicknamed **New Road** because it was built on the ruins of a severe earthquake in 1934. Here you can buy medicines, have film developed and, in the supermarket at the far end, find the variety of necessities you'd expect in a Western emporium. New Road leads directly to **Durbar Square** and the royal palace at the entrance to Old Kathmandu.

The Licchavi kings founded the city as Kantipur in the 8th century and laid the foundations of the Hanuman Dhoka Durbar, the palace which gives this area its name. The present compound was begun by Malla kings in the 1500s and enlarged by Prithvi Narayan Shah the Great after 1768. The building stands in the heart of a living museum of Malla dynasty architecture.

Flanking the brick palace with its broad-lintelled, latticed windows and nine-storey tower is the raised brick platform of **Basantapur Chowk**, where the royal elephants were kept and now a plaza where curio dealers spread their wares. **"Freak Street"**, leading off this space, was **37**

The Living Goddess

Kumari simply means "virgin" in Nepali, and the living goddess ceases to be regarded as divine upon reaching puberty. She is installed at the age of four or five after passing a series of tests that include being unafraid when locked in a dark room with howling masked demons and surrounded by the bloody heads of sacrificed animals.

Though she is considered to be the incarnation of Shiva's wife Parvati in her form as Taleju, patron deity of Hindu royalty, the Kumari is always selected from a Newari Buddhist family. During the festival of *Indra Jatra* in September the king visits the Kumari's house to pay homage and receive from her the red *tika* mark on his forehead. She can leave her quarters only seven times a year. Then she is carried through the town, heavily made up and costumed, to assure Kathmandu of her protection.

According to one of several legends, it all began with a girl who was exiled by a king for claiming to be the Kumari. When his queen thereupon became ill, the king brought the girl back and recognized her claim.

There are other Kumaris in towns and villages of the Kathmandu Valley. The one in the capital is known as the "Royal Kumari".

once the hub of the hippie culture and is now lined with shops for trekking gear and coloured jackets.

At the far end of this plaza stands the **Kumari Bahal**, house of the living goddess, guarded by painted lions with long wavy hippie-style hair. The courtyard of the three-storey building can be visited and, if enough rupees are collected, the Kumari herself may appear briefly at a beautifully carved upstairs window. The structure was built for the Kumari in 1757.

Try to ignore the wing of the palace across from the Kumari's house. The incongruous white Grecian façade was built in 1908 by Prime Minister Chandra Shumshere, a Rana responsible for the Singha Durbar and many of the city's neoclassical edifices. Continue past the high pagoda Vishnu temple, guarded by a splendid kneeling Garuda, to the **Kasthamandap**. The word means "House of Wood" and may have given

The Living Goddess is trained not show emotion, even if a fly lands on her nose.

38

Kathmandu its name. The latest building on the site is a rather squat 17th-century structure said to have been made from the wood of a single tree. It shelters a carmine-powder-encrusted image of the guru Gorakhnath in the midst of pigeons pecking at rice grains left as offerings.

To one side of the Kasthamandap is a small, shiny, brass-roofed enclosure dedicated to **Ganesh**. A constant procession of men and women break stride as they hurry along to touch a pillar of the shrine or reach up to sound the bells hanging from the low roof. Ringing bells at temples is a way of telling the god to pay attention to a prayer.

Turning back into Durbar Square, climb the nine steep steps of the central **Maju Deval** pagoda to Shiva for a view over the palace and its surrounding temples. The broad steps are a favourite spot for reading and loafing in the sun. From this vantage point you can enjoy the charming sight of Shiva and his wife Parvati in painted wood looking amiably out of an upper window of the adjoining temple. Just beyond is the great bell, which used to be rung to call the populace for important announcements, accompanied

All Kathmandu's on stage with Royal Durbar Square for a set.

by the huge drums further along the promenade. The drums are now thumped once a year to mark the sacrifices of bullocks during the big *Dasain* festival in October.

There are something like 50 temples and shrines, great and small, in the Hanuman Dhoka area. The palace takes its name from the red-cloaked figure of **Hanuman** to the left of the main entrance. His face is virtually obscured by red paste; guides say it is to spare him the sight of the goings-on—more acrobatic than erotic—carved on the struts of the small **Jaganath Temple** opposite.

When this bit of mythology is related, it immediately sends tour groups trotting across to see what is forbidden to the monkey god. Some say the carvings are there for pro- **41** tection, because the goddess of lightning is a virgin who would not come near anything so shocking. The erotica is probably best explained, however, along with Shiva's *lingam* phallus and the female *yoni* symbol, as an expression of the creative energy in male-female relations and the pleasure principles of Tantrism.

In the palace wall beyond the Hanuman statue and protected by a wooden fence is a **poem** in 15 languages etched in stone dated 14 January 1664. It is attributed to King Pratap Malla, reputed to be a great linguist. English appears in one word, "winter", and French with "l'hiver".

The **palace** itself is still used for the coronation of kings and for observance of religious rituals by the royal family. Like most other national museums, it opens at 10 a.m. and is closed on Tuesdays. Just inside the entrance is a remarkable 1673 sculpture in black stone of Vishnu as Narsingha, the man-lion, disembowelling a demon with the relish of a workman opening his lunchbox.

The inner courtyard, the **Nasal Chowk**, one of the few that can be visited, has curious and fine carved struts and door ornamentation. Binoculars are great for isolating such works of art from their busy surroundings and for appreciating the details of craftsmanship.

From here you can climb to the top of the **Basantapur Tower** and look down on the rooftops of Old Kathmandu. One wing of the palace houses a **museum** of relics of King Tribhuvan. It is like a walk-in scrapbook, with framed snapshots, newspaper clippings and memorabilia, such as the king's goldfish tank, bicycle and record player. A numismatic museum adjoins.

Back in Durbar Square, pigeons swirl constantly around one of Kathmandu's most colourful shrines, the **Kala** (Black) **Bhairav**. This is Shiva in his "destroyer" outfit, fanged and bedecked with skulls. The image acted as a sort of ancient lie detector, as it was said that anyone failing to tell the truth before it would bleed to death. Suspected criminals were brought here to force them to confess. However, the chocolate-faced god is quite gaily decorated with poster hues of red, yellow and blue, and his round, white-circled eyes look more startled than fierce. Nearby, behind a screened window, is the **Seto** (White) **Bhairav**, a gold-lacquered face through which beer spurts for scrambling devotees during *Indra Jatra*.

Adjoining the palace is the magnificent temple dedicated in 1564 by King Mahendra Malla to **Taleju**. Only the royal family prays here. It is enclosed by a wall with a gaudy gate that is opened to the public once a year during the *Dasain* festival. The three-tiered brick pagoda has gilded roofing, is topped by a golden bell-shaped cupola and decorated under the eaves by a fringe of wind chimes. It stands on a raised platform, its profile stately against the sky.

Beyond the Taleju temple begins a famous narrow diagonal street of shops, open-air markets and shrines most typical of Old Kathmandu. It is so crowded with humanity, on foot and on assorted wheels, and is crammed with so many fascinating things for sale, that one risks overlooking the significant monuments along the way.

At the **Indra Chowk** junction, four dragon-lions snarl beside the unusual stairway entrance to the many-hued and balconied **Akash Bhairav**, housing a silver Bhairav image brought out on feast days.

At the next junction, **Kel Tole**, a modest gateway on the left leads to the important **Seto Machendranath Temple**. An example of the fusion of religions, the inner temple to this Bodhisattva is encircled by Buddhist prayer wheels, while Hindu images are mounted on pedestals.

The next major junction, **Asan Tole**, is larger and even busier than the ones preceding. Here is the heart of Old Kathmandu, the rice market and collection point for porters looking for jobs. You have to thread your way through heaps of vegetables and fruit sold by farm wives sitting cross-legged on the ground, all the while heeding the warning bells and cries of cyclists and side-stepping cows browsing on vegetable leaves.

Almost overwhelmed by this swirl of humanity, the **Annapurna Temple** in the righthand corner gleams with burnished brass. The metal belt hanging over the roof is a *pataka*, a sort of hotline to speed prayers heavenwards. The shrine contains a *kalash*, a silver pot symbolizing wealth, for Annapurna, a Nepali version of Shiva's Parvati, is goddess of abundance.

From Asan Tole turn sharp left into a backstreet past tea **43** shops and continue until the next main intersection. On your left, in the wall of the corner house, thousands of nails have been hammered into a piece of wood under a small image of **Vaisha Dev**, the toothache god. In case this remedy doesn't ease the pain, several street-level dentists and denture shops have set up close by.

Turn right at this intersection and then left where two lions flank a passage leading to a striking white Buddhist stupa in a large courtyard. This is the **Kathe Simbhu** temple, built in the mid-17th century in the style of Swayambhunath (see p. 45) as a service to devotees physically unable to climb up to that hilltop shrine. There are several masterpieces of sculpture here and a *bahal*, or monastery, one of 120 tucked away in courtyards of the city.

At this point, continuing your way to Tahitty Tole, you can walk north to the main intersection of **Thamel**, Kathmandu's lively, fast-spreading centre for trekkers and budget-conscious tourists. Good shops, trekking agencies, bicycle renters, bookstalls, curio stands, restaurants and guest houses line the way. Some guest houses have pleasant gardens, most are clean and all are amazingly inexpensive. Many have bulletin boards where trekkers leave messages for friends or advertise to share a hike.

From Thamel's centre you can return to your starting point by heading right, or east, past the Old Vienna Inn and on to a roundabout, back in the modern part of town, where you come to the **Kaiser Library**. This has nothing to do with the German emperors, but was built by Field-Marshal Kaiser (a distortion of the Nepali name Kesar) Shumshere Rana. The tall trees surrounding this building, which also houses parts of the Ministry of Education, are the daytime roost of a colony of large fruit bats that seem to trade places at dusk with flocks of birds. The library is kept in scores of unlocked steel cabinets where valuable documents are jumbled randomly with novels. There are revealing framed photographs of assorted Ranas, smartly dressed in tweed suits, neckties and polished boots, posing daintily atop huge rhinos, gaurs and tigers they have slain. Although deposed, there are plenty of Ranas still around. The queen is a Rana, as is the king's mother.

The royal family lives in the modern **Narayanhiti Palace** across the street, behind flagpoles bearing the world's only non-rectangular national flag. Nepal's is made of two superimposed triangular pennants with sun and moon emblems. The palace stands at the head of the wide **Durbar Marg** avenue leading south. Here are airline and travel agency offices, banks, quality shops, restaurants and leading hotels—the opposite pole of tourism from Thamel. Veer right at the end of Durbar Marg to return to the Rani Pokhari basin where this itinerary began.

Kathmandu Environs

Crowning a hilltop about 3 miles (5 km.) west of the city centre, the 2,000-year-old Buddhist shrine of **Swayambhunath** can be seen from all over the valley. A taxi can take you half-way up the hill, but it is more interesting to climb the 365 steps through a wooded park, as pilgrims do. Have a few coins ready for the crones who beat away marauding monkeys that will snatch anything within reach.

Rickshaw driver snatches moment of peace before entering the fray.

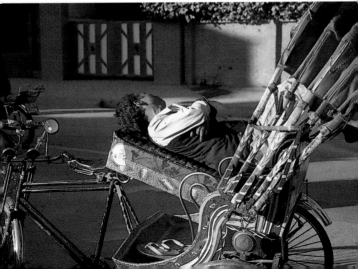

The steep stairs are lined with stone statuettes of animals and birds.

At the summit is one of the oldest stupas in the world, a swelling white mound surmounted by the astonishing all-seeing eyes of Buddha on four sides of a golden cube. Above this rises a tower of 13 diminishing golden disks symbolizing the 13 steps to enlightenment, then a golden royal parasol topped by a bell-shaped crown. Prayer flags stream on cords from the tower's pinnacle to the base, where prayer wheels ring the stupa. Monkeys and goats clamber about and forage for scraps of food offerings in small altars set in the stupa foundation. Always walk clockwise around the stupa, here and elsewhere.

The typical Nepali mix of Hinduism and Buddhism is again in evidence. Facing three pillars supporting finely wrought images of the White and Green Taras and a peacock is a very popular pagoda temple to a Hindu goddess who protects against smallpox and children's diseases. This temple, too, has Buddhist prayer wheels around it, worn shiny by turning hands. A small forest of white *chaitya* shrines and a porch where pilgrims congregate stands to one side of the stupa; on the other, at the head of the stairs, are two *shikara*-style votive towers to Hindu deities next to a large *dorje*, the tantric thunderbolt symbol.

Nearby, a **Tibetan monastery** is open to visitors. At 4 p.m. the monks can be observed at prayer, blowing the groaning horns and banging drums and cymbals in a red and gold chapel.

At sunset the terrace of Swayambhunath offers a fine view of Kathmandu and the bowl of the valley, as the tower burns red-gold. No matter how many tourists collect here, they are always outnumbered by pilgrims, who come from all over Asia to worship at this shrine.

On the road back to town, stop at the **National Museum** to admire its small but select collection of art and artefacts. Here are Licchavi stone reliefs of Shiva and Parvati from the 5th and 6th centuries, the classical period of sculpture. Figures are more slim and graceful than the commonly seen balloon-breasted models of the Mallas. A lovely 8th-

There's no escaping Buddha's all-seeing gaze on Swayambhunath.

century Birth of Buddha is curiously reminiscent of Christian nativity scenes. A great Bhairav urn and a comical terracotta Ganesh are noteworthy. The historical wing is filled with ancient weapons, including leather cannon that must have given gunners a few anxious moments. The adjacent Natural History Museum has done more for the moths of Nepal than for the sorry-looking stuffed birds and animals. The museum is closed on Tuesdays.

Bodhnath, 2½ miles (4 km.) on the other side of Kathmandu, is a stupa similar to the one at Swayambhunath,

Tibetan kids take a lighter view, while refugee elders pray.

but has a special magic because of its situation. The temple, constructed around A.D. 500, is encircled by monasteries, shops and lodges for pilgrims. It cannot be seen fully until you enter its precincts through a narrow passage from the street. Then it looms above you, 125 feet (38 m.) high, streamers of prayer flags fluttering gaily against the sky. It is possible to reach terraces around the dome by climbing a staircase guarded by painted, man-bearing stone

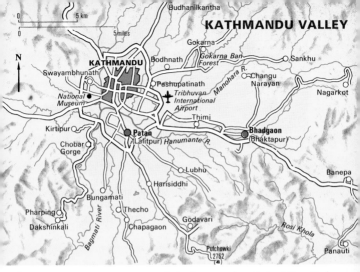

Budhanilkantha

Gokarna

Bodhnath
Gokarna Ban
Forest

Sankhu

KATHMANDU

Swayambhunath

Pashupatinath

Manohara R.

Changu
Narayan

National
Museum

Tribhuvan
International
Airport

Nagarkot

Kirtipur

Thimi

Patan
(Lalitpur) *Hanumante R.*

Bhadgaon
(Bhaktapur)

Chobar
Gorge

Banepa

Lubhu

Harisiddhi

Bungamati

Pharping

Thecho

Godavari

Rosi Khola

Dakshinkali

Chapagaon

Panauti

Bagmati River

Putchowki
2762

0   5 km

0   5miles

N

Nepal's Tibetans

Tibetan refugees poured into Nepal and India after China annexed their country in 1950, and now form a dynamic and colourful element in Nepalese society. There are perhaps 35,000 persons of Tibetan birth in the country, a third of them in the Kathmandu Valley and others in mountain villages and the vicinity of Pokhara. Their carpet industry is a major money-earner for Nepal, as is the foreign exchange tourists use to buy prayer wheels, brass "singing bowls" and knitwear made by refugees or imported from Tibet. Foreign governments, especially Switzerland and West Germany, have helped the refugees land on their feet. Refugee "camps", such as Jawalakhel near Patan and Hyangja outside Pokhara, are really not so much camps as thriving Tibetan communities.

Long before the events of 1950, Tibetans had settled in Nepal. The stupas at Swayambhunath and Bodhnath are flanked by Tibetan *gompas*, monasteries established long ago at sites venerated by Buddhists. The Dolpo and Lopa peoples of the remote border valleys, such as Mustang, are pure Tibetan, while related mountain tribes, notably the Sherpas, migrated from Tibet centuries ago.

49

elephants. The all-seeing eyes here seem genuinely penetrating, almost glowering above the whitewashed dome. The question mark "nose" is actually the Nepali numeral one, meaning the only way to enlightenment is by following the rules of conduct laid down by the Buddha.

Bodhnath has attracted Tibetan monks for centuries, and a Tibetan and Sherpa community has grown up in this village. Pilgrims coming from Tibet, as well as local refugees, supply the shops that ring the stupa with the best selection of Tibetan silver ornaments, long, telescoping copper horns and prayer wheels, brass "singing bowls", fur hats and other garments. Where Swayambhunath is cluttered with monuments in different styles, Bodhnath is pure and stands alone in the intimate embrace of its devotees.

The principal shrine to Shiva, patron of Nepal, reveres him as Pashupati, Lord of the Beasts. **Pashupatinath**, located on the Bagmati River near the airport, is one of the most sacred spots for Hindus. The great temple complex can only be entered by Hindus, but views of its huge golden Nandi bull (five times life size) and massive embossed silver doors can be had from the terrace and wooded hill across the river. From a bridge you can look down on the funeral ghats, and there is no objection to photography. There is usually a cremation in progress on one of the platforms by the river. The ashes will be scattered in the stream, regarded as holy because it is a tributary of the Ganges.

The river is also where on many occasions during the year the faithful take ritual purification baths. Purity being somewhat difficult to conceive as achievable in these polluted waters, the government is now planning to clean up the Bagmati.

Neglected by tour guides, but beautiful in decay, is the nearby walled enclosure of **Panchamukhi Mahadev**, with trees growing from the tops of its five white temple towers. The outbuildings now serve as a government shelter for the homeless aged, helped by the contributions of visitors and by Mother Teresa's organization.

At Bodhnath, it's no sacrilege to have fun climbing on the stupa.

Patan *(Lalitpur)*

Patan easily lives up to its early name, Lalitpur, meaning "Beautiful City". The monuments of the rose-red town with the golden roofs are the pinnacle of Newari craftsmanship. Unlike Kathmandu, it has no modern section or business district. It is rather like a rural town, with farming families drying grain and chillies on mats beside temples and in front of their houses. With the exception of the Pulchowk district just across the Bagmati River from the capital, where the offices of the United Nations, bilateral aid agencies, and several good hotels are situated, old Patan has changed little over the centuries. It is still largely contained in the boundaries marked by four grassy mounds called Ashoka stupas after the Indian monarch who visited Nepal in 250 B.C., married his daughter to a local prince, and may have had these mounds erected.

On **Durbar Square** stands the low, brick Deotalli Durbar palace and facing it eight temples crowded into a relatively small space. Several are of the Indian *shikara* steeple design; and one, the **Krishna Mandir**, built by King Siddhi Narasingha Malla in 1636, is of Moghul inspiration and, unusual for Nepal, is constructed entirely of stone. Its two lower storeys have a remarkable carved frieze representing scenes from the *Mahabharata* and *Ramayana* epics. This kind of story-telling was an important way to perpetuate legends for illiterate devotees, like comic books in stone. A golden Garuda in his usual *namaste* pose kneels on a pillar before the temple.

A bit farther on, a higher **column** holds the gilded image of King Yoganarendra Malla (1684–1705) seated on a throne and unperturbed by the cobra's hood hovering over him. Atop this is a bronze bird like those found on the corners of temple roofs. This king once told his people that as long as such birds did not fly away, his spirit would remain in the valley.

And so to the **Deotalli Durbar** itself and another masterpiece of the square, the 17th-century **Golden Gate**, depicting Shiva and his Parvati over the doorway to one of the palace's three interior courtyards. The first and smallest of these, **Sundari Chowk,** encloses a glorious royal tub, entered by steps and encrusted with intricate sculptures. The

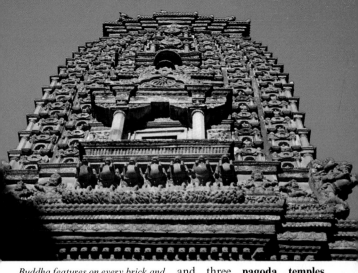

Buddha features on every brick and tile of Mahaboudha Temple.

tank is encircled by small sculptured deities and coiled snakes. In the next courtyard, **Mul Chowk**, are two outstanding examples of Newari metalwork, tall bronze reliefs of the goddesses Ganga and Jamuna standing on a crocodile and a tortoise respectively. Over the door, Surya, the Apollo-like sun god, rides in a chariot drawn by seven prancing horses, an animal rarely seen in Nepali art.

A huge bell that has no rope (its clapper is swung by hand) and three **pagoda temples** stand outside the palace. The closest, a Shiva shrine, has erotic carvings at the base of its struts. The farthest pagoda is dedicated to a local god, Bhimsen, patron of merchants and dear to Newars. Some art historians state that the pagoda style originated in Nepal and was taken to China and beyond by the master Patan artisan Arniko. He was invited to Tibet to cast bells and design stupas in the 13th century. He later took a group of Newari craftsmen to Peking and remained at the court of the Ming emperor as an important official. No examples **53** of his work survive in Nepal.

Leaving the square at this point you descend a lane past several decaying temples with grass growing from their tiles and come to the five-tiered **Kumbeshwar** pagoda to Shiva founded in 1392. Two ponds in the temple compound are said to be fed by waters from the holy Gosainkund Lake in the Himalayas. During summer, thousands of devotees come to bathe in these ponds beneath a richly ornamented Shiva *lingam*.

The lane parallel to the one you came down leads up to a hidden jewel, the **Kwa Bahal**, a Buddhist monastery founded in the 11th century and enclosing the **Golden Temple**. Two white-painted lions mark the entrance. Inside, the monastery surrounds a sunken courtyard with an exquisite golden shrine in the centre, backed by a pagoda temple decorated with episodes from the life of Buddha. Two bronze elephants standing on tortoises with riders in prayer flank the steps leading to the courtyard. Strands of prayer flags loop from the beaks of birds on the upturned roof corners of the shimmering golden shrine.

The alleys of Patan will lead to a succession of half-hidden temples and shrines of great beauty and interest. One of the most impressive is the **Mahaboudha**, or Temple of the Thousand Buddhas, erected in the 16th century. Designed after the temple at Bodh Gaya in India where Buddha reached enlightenment, this soaring spire boasts an image of Buddha on each one of its bricks. Extensively damaged during the 1934 earthquake, it has been faithfully reconstructed by Newari artisans.

The road from Kathmandu to Patan through Pulchowk passes an Ashoka stupa and brings you to **Jawalakhel** and the Tibetan Cooperative. Founded in 1960 with Swiss assistance for Tibetan refugees, this centre makes carpets and other goods for sale. In surrounding buildings the process of carding, washing and spinning wool, dyeing it and weaving the carpets can be followed from start to finish. A number of children can be seen squatting at the looms. The legal age for child labour in Nepal is 12. Quality of carpets is judged by the number of knots per square inch—60, 80 or (superlative) 100. Profits of the cooperative

Patan's royalty held court in the 17th-century Mul Chowk.

go to support schools and help handicapped and aged Tibetan refugees.

Farther on, at the **Patan Industrial Estate**, Newari craftsmen can be watched carving windows and door frames for reconstruction projects or boxes for the tourist trade. They use the same tools and methods as their ancestors and demonstrate the same skills. So do the workers in bronze, who cast figurines by the ancient "lost wax" method. Shops here offer good value. The artisans are not faking antiques; they are continuing traditions.

A Disappearing Heritage

While you won't see guards at every temple (there are simply too many shrines), they are a necessity. A great deal of Nepali art has vanished from the country to end up in museums and private collections abroad. This organized thievery is still going on, for there are some 2,500 temples in the Kathmandu Valley alone, almost 900 of them classified by Unesco as artistically important. A frequent sight on a day's ramble is a lovely sculpture lying half-buried by a wayside shrine. Chances are it will not be there long at the rate such art works are being smuggled out.

Bhadgaon *(Bhaktapur)*

Bhadgaon lies 10 miles (16 km.) east of the centre of Kathmandu and is served by trolley buses installed with Chinese aid. Its old name, Bhaktapur, means "City of the Faithful", and this could today be taken to mean loyalty to the old ways, for Bhadgaon is even more medieval than Old Kathmandu or Patan. Exploring its sloping streets you'll come upon squares filled with pottery drying in the sun and potters working at their hand-spun wheels, weavers at their looms and wood-carvers at work on window frames or making the *saranghi*, a kind of violin, or drums in all sizes. Artists with the finest of brushes paint the infinitely detailed stylized religious designs called *thangkas*. These are widely sold, but the best come from Bhadgaon.

Everyday household items —metal or clay vessels, winnowing baskets, rope, rough black peasant wrap-around skirts with a red hem, the short hoes used in rice paddies, plough blades and handles—just about everything is

Old skills survive, for temple repairs or carving souvenirs.

still made here by hand. Bhadgaon is home to many of the Newari families who work the fields that come right up to the city's edge.

Bhadgaon has its share of remarkable monuments, too. If the **Durbar Square** seems less crowded than in other cities, it's because it suffered most in the 1934 earthquake. Empty platforms show where temples once stood. Others have been painstakingly restored in an on-going cooperation between Nepal and West German experts, making use of the undiminished skills of the local craftsmen.

At the centre of the square is the **Tripura Durbar**, founded in the 15th century and better known as the Palace of 55 Windows. King Bhupatindra Malla, who embellished the square in the 18th century, looks down from his pillar onto the glorious **Sun Dhoka**, the Golden Gate, which serves as entrance to the palace. The gateway surpasses anything of its kind in the valley and was created at the height of Malla development in 1753. The ten-armed goddess in the centre of the *torana* is Taleju, pulling the hair of a demon beneath a pot-bellied Garuda and assorted writhing snakes and cavorting attendants. The

gate is topped with the double pennants from which the Nepal national flag is derived.

Inside, workmen are restoring a **temple to Taleju** that is closed to non-Hindus, but you can admire the carving on its door and get a peek past the attendant soldier to the ornate interior.

The **art museum** adjoining the Palace of 55 Windows contains a collection of antique *thangkas* and sculpture in wood and stone. At the far end of the royal mall is a *shikara*-style **temple to Durga**, interesting for the pairs of animals guarding the stairs.

A short street of shops descending from the far corner of the square, behind a 15th-century replica of the Pashupatinath temple (see p. 50), leads to Taumadi Tole. This square is dominated by Bhadgaon's most famous monument, the **Nyatapola Temple**, highest in the valley and one of only two five-tiered pagodas. Beginning with a pair of burly mustachioed Malla wrestlers, the staircase is lined with animal guardians, at each level ten times stronger than the one below. The pagoda's 108 painted struts support the five tiled roofs. What's inside, nobody knows. The door has not been opened

Bhadgaon's Peacock Window is for looking out, not in.

since the temple was consecrated in 1702.

Facing the temple is a teahouse of several storeys with balconies where one can eat while watching the animated marketing of chickens and goats in one corner of the square and admire the **Akash Bhairava Temple**'s crop of healthy weeds sprouting from the roof tiles. This is the home of the little Bhairav idol paraded in his chariot during the *Bisket* New Year's festival.

Duck through a low passage between two shops across the street to find the **Til Mahadev Narayan Temple** in an untouristy rubble-filled square where there are families washing, goats looking out of upstairs windows and, behind a grill in a small kiosk, a *lingam* much venerated by older women who keep it covered with flowers. The *lingam* is watered by a continuous drip from an overhead jar.

Bhadgaon expanded over the centuries from a nucleus around the **Tachupal Tole**, reached by a walk from the Nyatapola Temple through narrow streets full of unfamiliar merchandise: the lengths **59** of red yarn are sold to be plaited in women's hair; the grey cannon balls are home-made soap; the conical yellowish cigarettes are *bidi*, the cheapest tobacco, and can be bought singly. There will be heaps of orange turmeric, cardamom, ginger and other spices and bundles of dried fish, looking like twigs. *Pan* sellers offer to mix lime, spices and bits of nuts and tobacco in a fresh betel leaf packet for chewing. Bigger leaves stuck together with bamboo toothpicks are sold as plates for temple offerings.

Many of the old houses around Tachupal Tole have been very carefully restored. At one end is the **Dattatraya Temple**, used impartially by Buddhists and Hindus. Two large wrestlers, symbolic of the first Malla, a strongman, flank the open porch of this structure, and a gilded Garuda kneels on a column above. In an alley just off the square is the famous **Peacock Window** of delicately carved wood. It is in a former priest's house, Pujahari Math, now used as a government office.

Bhadgaon's treasures are many, and if time permits you will be amply rewarded by allowing two half-days to wandering through its alleys.

Kathmandu Valley

Just minutes away from the heart of Kathmandu, life goes on as it has for centuries in the rural communities of the valley. Most of the network of motorable roads is less than 30 years old. Before that there were few cars in Nepal. In the valley, at least the main street of principal villages is paved and accessible by taxi and bus, though the slower pace of walking or cycling is the most pleasant way to enter this world where time seems to have stopped.

Farmland begins at the very edge of the cities, and the fields are full of activity whatever the season. Rice needs lots of water, so the paddy (the shoots are grown from seed) is transplanted when the June rains flood the fields. This is a job for the women, working in lines to space the young plants in neat rows. In summer the rice forms a green velvety blanket, then turns golden in autumn when it ripens and is harvested. This brings out the whole valley, bending low with small sickles to cut the stalks and stacking these in

Men and women separate to offer gifts at Kali's bloody shrine.

sheaves for fuel or thatch after the rice is threshed. Then the grain is dried in the sun, covering the squares and streets of villages, and is winnowed by tossing in the air from round trays. Fields of yellow mustard are grown for oil-seed. Wheat is planted as a winter crop in the paddies, and garden plots supply maize, chillies and vegetables.

The ruminative buffalo pulls ploughs and carts, then wallows in the mud of a village pond. Chickens run in and out of doorways and often may be seen peering out from roosts on the second floor of houses. Under the eaves bundles of maize hang to dry along with large cucumbers. Pumpkin vines climb over rooftops.

Another winter crop is bricks. The topsoil is neatly set aside, the clay beneath is dug out for brick-making and the fertile black earth is then replaced. Bricks fired on the spot are the valley's main building material.

Saturday is a good day to visit **Dakshinkali** (a 40-minute drive from Kathmandu to the southern end of the valley), when many pilgrims bring chickens and goats to sacrifice to Kali. Sacrifices also take place on Tuesday.

The shrine is at the bottom of a shady glen by a brook. Carrying their offerings by the feet (incidentally, only male animals may be sacrificed), women form a line on one side and men on the other. The altar where the blood will be spilled is out of sight behind a wall where a loudspeaker screeches hymns to Kali. Under a bridge a witches' cauldron bubbles. Decapitated fowl are chucked in to speed the plucking and goats are seared to remove the hair. The offal is thrown into the stream.

Along the banks, barbecues convert the sacrifices into lunch. Some picnickers say they're doing the animal a favour, giving it a chance of a better reincarnation. A thriving souvenir market lines the path to the parking lot.

On the way back towards Kathmandu, the village of **Pharping** deserves a stop. It is untouched by tourism and has many beautifully carved windows in mud brick houses gently crumbling away. A path leads uphill to two Tibetan monasteries and a temple to the **Bajra Yogini**, a local

Tucked away off Pharping road, Buddhist hermitage is ideal spot for meditation.

deity, guarded by bronze lions and a small waggly dog.

Beyond Pharping, turn off to see the **Chobar Gorge** of the Bagmati River created by the sabre of Manjushri (see p. 16). It is indeed scarcely wider than a sword slash, crossed by a miniature iron suspension bridge brought from Scotland and portered in at the turn of the century. Below, the **Jal Binayak** temple to Ganesh stands by the rocks where women do laundry and chil-

Even when clouds obscure Everest, Pulchowki affords tremendous views.

dren dive, while a funeral ghat stands mercifully downstream from these activities. On the wall here, you'll see what appears to be the Star of David. This is a Hindu emblem of two superimposed triangles, the up-pointing one denoting the male force, the other the female. A bronze rat, Ganesh's companion, fronts the

losses, he punished the local population by cutting off the noses and lips of all men except those who played wind instruments.

In the middle of the town is the **Bagh Bhairav Temple** with swords and shields from the 18th-century siege under its eaves. A climb through the streets takes you past many open doorways where women work the treadles of their clattering hand looms, the most important local industry.

From the restored **Uma Maheshwar Temple** at the highest point there is a fine view of the valley and two stone elephants with spikes on their backs to prevent kids from playing *mahout*. Instead, the kids will probably be found playing "Goats and Tigers", a favourite national game that can be marked out in chalk on the ground and played with pebbles, or on attractive brass boards with carved pieces. Girls like to play jacks with pebbles. Popular, too, is a kind of billiards played by flicking checkers on a square board.

The highest peak on the valley's rim is **Pulchowki**, 9,062 feet (2,762 m.), a half-day trip beyond Patan through verdant scenery rising to the attractive village of

temple, looking very like a dachshund. A cement factory belching smoke is a regretted addition to this corner of the valley.

Off the road back to the capital lies the valley's fourth most important town, **Kirtipur**. King Prithvi the Great had difficulty conquering Kirtipur, whose site atop a ridge with two high points made it virtually impregnable. When he finally succeeded after a prolonged siege and heavy

65

Godavari. The road up Pulchowki is gravel or worse much of the way and is only motorable during the dry season. The hiking trail takes a good three hours, passing through rhododendrons, orchids and laurel. At the top, the breathtaking mountain view on a clear morning sweeps from Kanchenjunga and Everest to the Annapurnas.

Godavari's **Royal Botanical Gardens** at the foot of the mountain has an orchid collection, lovely trees and a brook. It is a favourite haunt of bulbuls, barbets and the orange-bellied chloropsis, as well as those who understand this language—bird-watchers. A hundred species of butterfly have been identified here as many different birds.

Other country roads running south from Patan pass two- and three-storeyed narrow brick houses bunched close together in the Newari fashion. A stroll through any of these hamlets, **Bungamati**, **Thecho** or **Chapagaon**, will provide intimate glimpses of country life. Stroll with care, however—the back paths are heavily fertilized by humans as well as by animals.

Thimi, on the road from Kathmandu to Bhadgaon, is where papier-mâché masks are made and sold. On this road, too, are potteries that make attractive flowerpots in the shape of elephants and other creatures. Thimi's streets often become open-air kilns when pots are fired beneath smoldering rice straw. Festivals in these villages, if you can find the right day and hour, are even more riotous and welcoming than those in the cities.

The road north from Kathmandu leads about 5 miles (8 km.) to **Budhanilkantha** and the giant statue of Vishnu reclining on a bed of snakes. Carved from one black stone and set in a sunken tank of water, the 16-foot (5-m.) image dates from the 7th century. The legend goes that as Vishnu floated partly submerged in the primeval ocean, a lotus grew out of his navel, issuing Brahma whose sole task was to create the world. The king cannot visit this shrine, as to look upon what is considered to be an image of himself, an incarnation of Vishnu, would be a forecast of death. On festival days worshippers blanket the statue

Vishnu sleeps on, undisturbed by birds above, snakes below.

with flowers. Beyond is **Shivapuri Peak**, a popular one-day trek with good mountain vistas.

If you can't see a tiger any other way, you can be sure to get a glimpse of one and perhaps two at the privately owned 650-acre (260-hectare) **Safari Park** at Gokarna. The park is beyond Bodhnath, a half-hour drive from Kathmandu in a walled royal forest. Let purists sniff, this isn't as contrived as it sounds. The park is a well-preserved patch of forest. You can take a one-hour elephant ride on jungly trails and see many birds and deer. The tigers are fenced off in a large corner of the park, big enough for them to stay out of each other's way. A live bait is put out at night during the peak tourist season, depending on the number of people signing up for the experience. As the manager explained it, "We put out a goat for seven or eight people and a young buffalo if there are 20 people. If we ever get a hundred people we'll throw in a guide."

The park bus provides transportation for tiger-viewers to and from their hotels. The park also has a nine-hole golf course and 100 beehives belonging to the king, possibly manufacturing royal queen bee jelly around the clock for the palace.

If one spot outside the cities is a must, it is **Changu Narayan**. The oldest temple in the valley and unquestionably one of the most interesting, it sits on an isolated hilltop a few miles north of Bhadgaon and just south of the Gokarna road. Many people like to walk up through rice fields from the Gokarna side. The drive from Bhadgaon also cuts across paddies and climbs past thickets of bamboo to the ridge top. A misty morning makes the scene even more evocative of the past.

The temple is in the centre of a walled enclosure with a treasury of small sculptures and shrines dotted about. One of several masterpieces dedicated to the cult of Vishnu is a broken 8th-century stone panel, a Licchavi work. There is a lovely 5th-century Garuda and near it, on a memorial pillar, the earliest historical document in Nepal, an inscription of the same period concerning the Licchavi King Manadeva. Doors, niches, struts and cornices are superbly decorated, yet the temple and compound retain a human dimension and are not overwhelming.

Beyond the Valley

From Kathmandu, short trips just outside the valley make it possible for those who haven't got time to go farther to see the high mountains at sunrise or sunset.

Nagarkot, less than an hour from Bhadgaon by car, is on the crest of a ridge at 7,111 feet (2,168 m.). You reach it after driving up a winding road amid some hopeful signs of pine-tree reforestation. The last bit to the observation tower takes 10 minutes on foot. From there the Himalayas rear up as if they were magnified by a telephoto lens, with little depth in between. There are a number of small guest houses where one spends the night to see sunset and/or sunrise, neither being guaranteed except in the clear ether of winter.

The road from Bhadgaon to **Dhulikhel**, a mountain town south-east of Nagarkot, passes through Banepa, where you can turn off to visit **Panauti**. The buildings here have great artistic importance but are falling apart. They give an

Little Red Riding Hood, Nepal style, and hill-tribe pals.

On Top of the World

Long before a British mapping team in 1852 declared 29,028-foot (8,848-m.) "Peak XV" to be the highest spot on earth and named it after Surveyor General Sir George Everest, the people of Nepal recognized the supremacy of their mountain. They call it "Sagarmatha", Mother of the Universe. This isn't so exaggerated, since the high mountains feed the headwaters of the Ganges and Brahmaputra rivers, bringing life to hundreds of millions in Nepal, India and Bangladesh.

The first organized attempt to reach the summit was made from the Tibetan side in 1922. Why climb it? "Because it's there," was the classic answer of British mountaineer George Mallory, who disappeared into the clouds near the top on his fatal second attempt from Tibet in 1924. Twenty-nine years later New Zealander Edmund Hillary and Tenzing Norgay Sherpa made it from Nepal, and since then more than 200 climbers from some 20 countries have accomplished the feat. Mrs Junko Tabei of Japan was the first woman to stand on the top of the world, in 1975, and another Japanese, Yuichiro Miura, was the first to ski back down, in 1970. Nowadays, climbers seek their firsts by attempting new and difficult routes and methods. Reinhold Messner from the South Tyrol area of Italy, the greatest of modern mountaineers, has climbed Everest twice without oxygen, once in a solo four-day dash. Two Sherpas have climbed it five times. By the end of 1988, 95 persons had died while making the attempt to conquer Mount Everest, including 40 Sherpas. The climb may only be undertaken with government permission and on payment of a not-too-substantial fee.

The mountain dominates the Sagarmatha National Park, formed in 1976 with assistance from New Zealand. This park, covering an area of 480 square miles (1,243 sq. km.), is also a World Heritage Site, and boasts a wide variety of fauna and flora, the former including musk deer, Himalayan tahr, red panda, black bear, wolves, marmots and snow leopard. And most elusive of all—the yeti! Sir Edmund Hillary, now New Zealand's Ambassador to India and Nepal, has created a Himalaya Foundation that has helped build schools, hospitals, bridges and electrification projects for Sherpa villages in the area.

Most Himalayan snow falls before reaching high and dry Everest.

idea of what many of the valley cities looked like before the restorers went to work. Dhulikhel's mountain view is different from Nagarkot's but is equally spectacular. There is an attractive resort hotel with brick cottages and flowered walks nestled into the mountainside. The restaurant is good, too, which is rare outside the capital. When sunset comes, the mountains are first pink, then rapidly turn a frosty grey.

Before dawn next morning you are led to the top of the hill to watch the darkness give way to a glow silhouetting another stretch of the Himalayas range, then flare into light that gilds a hundred snowy peaks.

The road beyond Dhulikhel drops precipitously, then turns up the Sun Kosi River gorge towards the Chinese-Tibetan border. After the hot-spring town of **Tatopani**, the walls of the gorge draw closer and closer to the road until the customs post at **Kodari** is reached. A Chinese visa obtainable in Kathmandu is required to enter Tibet. Four-day bus tours from Kathmandu to Lhasa and the Tibetan Plateau are becoming a popular excursion for visitors to Nepal. Unfortunately, landslides often close the highway.

Some 124 miles (200 km.) west of the capital by road and half-an-hour by air is **Pokhara**, a major staging point for treks and the fastest-growing city in the country. Almost as spectacular as the flight to Everest, the air route heads in the opposite direction and parallels the high mountains towards Annapurna. Below, all signs of roads are gone, and it is clear how difficult road-building is in this tortuous terrain. The approach to Pokhara skims in through a narrow pass. The town, at 3,000 feet (900 m.) is almost tropical, with banana and jacaranda trees, papayas and cactus. The contrast makes the stunning views of snow-capped **Macchapuchhare,** the famous "Fish Tail" peak dubbed the "Nepalese Matterhorn", all the more marvellous.

Pokhara is on **Lake Phewa**. The lakeside part of town is where Westerners congregate to rent bikes, shop for Tibetan wares that are cheaper here than in the capital and breakfast on fresh fruit juice and muesli. On the airport side there are several good hotels, one on the lake reached by a barge. There is much bustle as

Macchapuchhare's snow waters Pokhara's tropical vegetation.

trekking groups arrive or depart. Day walks, up **Sarangkot** to see Dhaulagiri from the viewing tower, to the Tibetan camp at Hyangja or the spooky limestone **Mahendra Cave** are fun. You can also take a boat on the lake or walk out to **Devin's Fall** where a river disappears underground into a steamy hole. Overnight camping trips can be arranged for those unable to take a real trek. But Pokhara is a beautiful spot where it can be quite enough just to relax and enjoy the mountain scenery in warm sunshine.

The road back to Kathmandu follows the Seti River for much of the way. A new side road makes it now easy to visit **Gorkha**, ancestral seat of the Shah dynasty. The drive into the smiling Gorkha Valley is alone worth the trip. The town is preparing for tourists but does not yet have many amenities. A large Shah palace there is being restored by wood-carvers, and you can climb for half an hour up to the stronghold of Prithvi the Great, now inhabited by priests. Looking out of a window onto the panorama of **73**

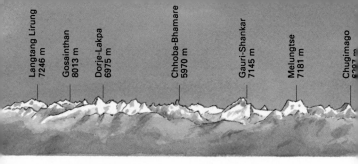

Langtang Lirung 7246 m
Gosainthan 8013 m
Dorje-Lakpa 6975 m
Chhoba-Bhamare 5970 m
Gauri-Shankar 7145 m
Melungtse 7181 m
Chugimago 6297 m

Flying over Everest

For a close-up view of Mount Everest and the Himalayan giants, take the Royal Nepal Airlines Mountain Flight. The plane takes off from Kathmandu daily and quickly climbs to 20,000 feet (6,000 m.) still below the level of the highest mountains, stretching as far as the eye can see. As you fly eastwards, you'll note that many have little or no snow, an exception being the first on your left, **Langtang Lirung**. Each passenger receives a profile of this section of the range identifying no less than 19 peaks above 18,000 feet (5,490 m.). The pilot will point these out and invites passengers, two at a time, to come into the cockpit for photography.

The peak of **Everest** appears as a black pyramid, buttressed by **Lhotse** and **Nuptse**, its summit tearing a white streamer of condensation from the stratospheric jet stream. After half an hour and just before reaching **Kanchenjunga** (28,208 feet or 8,598 m.) on the border

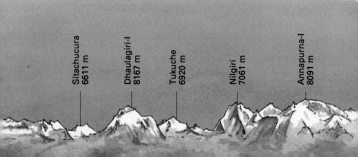

Sitachucura 6611 m
Dhaulagiri-I 8167 m
Tukuche 6920 m
Nilgiri 7061 m
Annapurna-I 8091 m

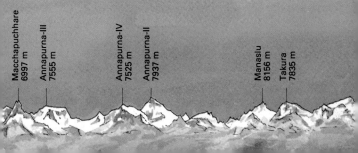

Kanchenjunga
8598 m →

Numbur 6956 m
Cho-Oyu 8153 m
Nuptse 7906 m
Everest 8848 m
Lhotse 8501 m
Ama-Dablam 6863 m
Makalu 8475 m

with Sikkim, the plane turns back, this time coming within 14 miles (23 km.) of Everest and skimming the tops of razor-edged ridges and sharp peaks of the massif. **Namche Bazar** and **Thyangboche Monastery** can be seen south of the flank of the Everest massif. Grey glaciers, turquoise lakes and the rust coloured plateau of Tibet beyond the mountains pass in review. The route followed by Edmund Hillary and Tenzing Norgay Sherpa is on the right side of Everest's pyramid as

you head back towards Kathmandu.

Almost as fascinating as the mountain vista is the face of Nepal unfolding beneath the aircraft: steep, red, eroded hillsides, the trails to passes to Tibet, the corrugation of endless terracing, the white rivers cutting through dark-shadowed gorges and the absence of roads over most of the landscape. It doesn't matter which side of the plane you sit on, for you'll get the same view, either on the outbound flight or the return journey.

Macchapuchhare 6997 m
Annapurna-III 7555 m
Annapurna-IV 7525 m
Annapurna-II 7937 m
Manaslu 8156 m
Takura 7835 m

Nepal's Fighting Men

"Gurkhas", Nepalese mercenaries, have served under the British flag since 1815. They are not a tribe, but come mainly from the Magar, Gurung, Limbu and Rai tribes of the central and eastern hill districts. They got their name from the Principality of Gorkha, whose troops unified Nepal in the 18th century. Soon afterwards these soldiers won the respect of the British by repelling their attempt to invade from India.

There are many tales about the bravery, toughness and loyalty of the Gurkhas. In 1890 one Lieutenant Swinton was killed when a bullet ricocheted off the hard head of his Gurkha orderly. The mountain men had never seen the ocean until sent to Europe during World War I. They wondered how the troop ships could find their way when "the trail is all behind us and nothing in front."

In World War II, Gurkhas distinguished themselves in hand-to-hand fighting with their curved *kukri* knives in North Africa, at Monte Cassino in Italy, and in Burma. Nine thousand Gurkhas died in that war and 23,655 were severely wounded. They earned 2,734 decorations and mentions for gallantry. Gurkhas have won 13 Victoria Crosses, Britain's highest military medal. After India gained independence, the Gurkha regiments were divided between the Indian and the British armies. Those with the British army have since seen service in the Falklands War, in Belize, Cyprus and the Congo. Gurkha units are currently stationed in Hong Kong. Pensions paid to retired Gurkhas are an important source of foreign exchange in Nepal.

high mountains and wave upon wave of rolling hills, one can imagine the young prince saying to himself "This must be my kingdom." It was here that unification began.

Until recently few tourists strayed from the Kathmandu-Pokhara-Everest-Chitwan focal points. Now it is possible to see something of the undeveloped west without walking three weeks to get there. The Tiger Tops management, who pioneered the jungle camps and rafting in Nepal, are the first to offer a tented camp at **Royal Bardia Wildlife Reserve** on the Karnali. There are tigers to be seen (with luck), jungle walks and drives, and rafting on the river, a paradise for bird-watchers. The Karnali gorge above **Chisopani** is especially beautiful and is noted for the size of the fighting mahseer carp taken by sport fishermen. All this may change before long. There are plans to dam the Karnali at this point, part of developing Nepal's greatest natural resource, hydro-electric power. The country's potential is something like 80 million kilowatts, with present production under 200,000 kilowatts.

The government intends to promote trekking in the west at **Lake Rara** and **Jumla** and in the east in the **Arun Valley** and Sikkim border region. At present these are strictly for self-sufficient trekkers, as there are few lodges or places to buy food on the trail. In the east, the lowlands are heavily populated, but the market towns hold little to interest the tourist.

At least you can breathe on the roof of Gorkha-Kathmandu bus.

🐾 Chitwan

Chitwan, "Heart of the Jungle" in Nepali, is a tangled tropical forest on the southern border with India. This is the haunt of the Bengal tiger, of a third of the world's population of rare one-horned rhino and of more than 400 species of bird. Amazingly, from elephant back at the jungle's edge you can see the snow-capped Himalayas, less than 100 miles (160 km.) away and looming like a foam-crested wave. (No country on earth has such a great range in altitude, from 500 feet [150 m.] to 2,028 feet [8,848 m.], the

On Chitwan jungle's edge, dusty sunset glows over Tharu village.

guests, Chitwan became a national park in 1973 and has been designated by Unesco as a World Heritage Site. The **Royal Chitwan National Park** is 360 sq. mi. (930 sq. km.) of magnificent first-growth trees —the tall hardwood sal, the kapok "silk-cotton" tree and the flame-of-the-forest, with their spectacular crimson February flowers—ferns, bamboo, huge vines that choke trees to death like a python. And there are real pythons, too. White-ruffed langur monkeys leap and swing in the treetops, sending flights of green parakeets screeching. In open glades, peacocks preen, and the shy, tiny barking deer, no taller than the peacocks, race away at an intruder's approach. It's a magical environment.

The best way to see the wildlife, and certainly the most fun, is swaying atop a silently padding elephant. Elephant grass along the several rivers in the park is so tall that only in this way can you spot the rhinos, the wild boar and other creatures which are used to elephants and do not run from them. With luck, you'll see a leopard draped indolently on a tree branch and perhaps a stately sambar stag. In winter, the gaur, the world's

summit of Everest.) And this pristine wildlife reserve is within easy reach by air and road from Kathmandu.

Once the private hunting ground of royalty and their

Tiger-Watching

Everyone wants to see a tiger, but tigers don't seem to reciprocate. They are hard to find. There are perhaps 90 in the Chitwan park, hunting in the dark and lying in thickets for most of the day. A large male may weigh over 500 pounds (250 kg.) and measure 10 feet (3 m.) from nose to tail tip. You can hear them roar at night and see their pug marks on the jungle trails, and now and then ride an elephant to find a tigress and cubs resting in the high grass.

Villagers whose fields adjoin the park mount guard, banging pots and drums at night, to scare off tigers and leopards, which kill cattle, and rhinos, which break fences and destroy crops. Each year, tigers and rhinos kill one or two villagers who enter the park to cut grass for thatch.

The Tiger Tops Jungle Lodge in Chitwan nightly stakes out young buffalo as bait. When a tiger is reported, guests hurry in silence, barefoot, to watch from behind a blind as the floodlit animal feeds. Tiger Tops also operates a lodge and tented camp in the Royal Bardia Wildlife Reserve on the Karnali River in western Nepal where tigers can be observed on a bait. Tigers are protected in the Royal Sukla Phanta Wildlife Reserve, a former hunting preserve in Nepal's south-western corner, where the Silent Safari jungle camp is located.

largest wild ox, 6 feet (1.8 m.) high at the shoulder, comes out of its hideaway in the Siwalik Hills on the park's southern edge in search of young grass. Delicate spotted deer, sloth bear, giant flying squirrels and civet cats are among the mammals the visitor may see.

Gaida Wildlife Camp and the **Tiger Tops Jungle Lodge** both have cabins and a tented camp inside the park. Gaida is the place to see some of the 400 one-horned rhinos that are Chitwan's pride. Both have their own elephants and staff of nature guides. A half-day is usually spent in dug-out canoes watching egrets, ospreys, storks, ibis, kingfishers, eagles and scores of other fascinating birds along the river and searching for the endangered gharial, a narrow-

Tharu girls get a ride from elephant handlers, while Gaida guests close in on a rare rhino.

jawed fish-eating crocodile, and its flesh-eating cousin, the huge marsh mugger. The rare, almost sightless freshwater dolphin may come up for a blow alongside your canoe. At day's end, campers compare notes around the bar and perhaps watch a group of men from a nearby Tharu village perform by firelight an intricate sword dance with sticks.

Along the park boundary and especially at **Sauraha** near park headquarters, some 40 lodges and inexpensive guest houses cater to tourists. Elephant rides, jeep tours and canoe trips can be arranged at the park entrance, where an interesting interpretation centre provides a history of the area and information about its ecology. One is reminded that in 1938, during a safari arranged for the British Viceroy of India, hundreds of elephants took part in a hunt that bagged 120 tigers, 38 rhino and 27 leopards. Today, 500 soldiers are stationed in the park to keep out poachers.

Package tours, with two or three nights in or near the park, are widely offered by travel agencies in Kathmandu. You can fly to a field near the park in half an hour, go by car or tourist bus in about six hours or ride the Trisuli River rapids on a raft almost to the park boundary in a day.

Travel by road provides a glimpse of the **Terai**, the well-watered farming zone that stretches the length of the country on its southern border with India. The Terai is an extension of the Ganges Plain.

Tharu
For many years the Tharu were the only tribe in the area because they were immune to the widespread malaria. In the late 1950s a U.S. AID programme wiped out the disease. As a result, tens of thousands of farmers from the overcrowded hill districts moved in. Two-thirds of the forest was cleared for agriculture. Chitwan was saved at the eleventh hour by establishment of the park. Some 22,000 Tharu were moved out of the protected zone. Although they benefit somewhat from the flow of visitors to the park, now numbering well over 35,000 a year, the Tharus remain rather disgruntled at being displaced.

A visit to the mud-and-wattle thatched houses of a Tharu village is part of most package-tour programmes. As you pass by, children will call "bye-bye". It has become the local word for white foreigners.

82

It's only about 25 miles (40 km.) wide, but a third of Nepal's population lives here, producing much of the nation's food.

A visit to **Lumbini**, birthplace of Gautama Buddha, can also be made in about three hours from Chitwan. (There are also flights from Kathmandu to Bhairawa, the nearest airfield, with a bus service to Lumbini.) The story goes that Buddha's mother gave birth to him under a tree in a garden at Lumbini, unable to get back in time to the palace, some 12 miles (20 km.) away. Marking the spot are the shrine of Maya Devi and a pillar commemorating the visit in 250 B.C. of the Indian emperor Ashoka, a zealous convert to Buddhism. Buddhist pilgrims from all over the world come to Lumbini, but the government's arrangements to expand accommodation are still in the planning stage.

The road north from the Terai to Kathmandu over the Mahabharat mountains through **Daman** is one of the most beautiful in the country. The road winds upwards, paralleling the freight ropeway. At Daman, over 7,000 feet (2,300 m.), an observation tower with a telescope looks out over the Himalayas, from Annapurna to Everest. Along the way, women of the Tamang tribe, with large gold ornamental ear buttons and rings in their noses, carry heavy loads of wood or fodder. The lush **Palung Valley**, sheltering a Newar community, with yellow mustard fields, green rice paddies, and clumps of orange marigolds around every house, marks the halfway point.

Then terraces of maize drop precipitously down the mountainside as the road descends to Naubise to join the Prithvi Rajmarg highway built by the Chinese in 1973. The remaining stretch, with bridges broken by landslides and the surface pocked with spine-jarring potholes, is one of the worst drives, and is heavily congested with trucks and buses. The latter are a fearsome sight, especially at holiday time. Bodies cling to the sides and are squeezed out of windows from a packed interior. On the roof, riders perched on baggage sway perilously on the curves.

Alas, it is a rough road visitors may have to endure more than once, for it is on the way from Kathmandu to Pokhara and also to the river-rafting launch points on the Trisuli River.

White-Water Adventure

For heart-in-the-mouth thrills it would be hard to beat white-water rafting on the tumultuous snow-fed rivers of Nepal. Starting in the 1970s, rafting has rapidly become an experience thousands of intrepid tourists add to their trekking trip or visit to the Chitwan jungles. Rafting enthusiasts come expressly for the unique setting of rivers that drop 17,000 feet (5,000 m.) from their mountain sources to the Ganges, roaring down some of the world's deepest gorges.

There are three kinds of rafting. Experts start way up white-water rivers, such as the Sun Kosi, and spend a week or more on the water, far from any roads. The only way out is downstream, running world-class rapids that challenge skill and stamina. Less experienced rafters and even neophytes can take a calmer trip of three or four days on the Seti and Trisuli rivers. They'll paddle hard through rapids while a guide steers, then coast along through spectacular scenery.

They'll camp in tents on sandy beaches, where meals are prepared by support staff following by van on roads that run along the river valleys. The one-day and half-day trips on these rivers can be exciting, too, but less arduous, as a skilled oarsman does the rowing. A van picks up the rafters downstream and drives them back to Kathmandu or on to Chitwan.

The rafts usually take six passengers, plus two or three guides. Everyone has a life jacket and helmet. Your essentials are packed in a water-tight drum, for you'll be soaked half of the time. Tennis shoes are good for hooking your feet under a deck rope as you paddle, since there is no other way to hold on when you hit the rapids. The knowledge that even the best of rafters sometimes capsize in these currents keeps the adrenalin flowing as fast as the river. And there is a slightly hysterical note of relief in the laughter that follows each successful passage of a raft-tossing stretch.

The Trisuli is "rapidly" becoming Nepal's most popular white-water rafting river among the adventurous. It's also an exciting way to make a day trip down to Chitwan.

Trekking

Trekking in the Himalayas, once the ultimate adventure, has become possible for ordinary mortals without, however, loss of the exhilaration and sense of achievement that comes from walking on the roof of the world. Moreover, on a trek you'll come close to the lives of the distinctly different hill tribes, gaining insights on Nepal only possible in this way.

It's difficult for outsiders to grasp that not only is most of Nepal still beyond the reach of roads but also that there are a lot of people up in those hills. Mountain trails take you to villages, not to wilderness, as they would in the Alps or the Rockies. And just about every village these days has a guest house of sorts offering refreshments, food and lodging. This has helped to widen the variety of easily accessible treks, to make trekking benefit local people and also to increase trekking's pressure on the environment. Official figures show that of 221,147 visitors in 1987, 36,164 listed trekking as the purpose of their visit. Since many don't bother to specify their plans, it is estimated that at least 50,000 actually hit the trail that year. Americans, British and West Germans lead the pack, in that order.

Planning and Preparation

There are three ways to trek. You can book through a private agency that will plan your itinerary and provide everything, from down jackets, sleeping bags, food and drink to *sirdar* (guide), cook and porters who will set up the tents at campsites. Or you can bring your own gear or rent it locally and hire the crew you need. Or you can travel light with just your backpack, finding food and lodging wherever you choose to stop. A luxury trek in the first category might cost as much as $50 (Rs 1,200) per day per person; going it alone can be done for $5 (Rs 120).

October and November are the most popular trekking months because they are warm, sunny and the trails are dry after the monsoon. December is good for low-level treks, though it will be getting cold higher up. The winter months bring the clearest skies. Spring comes in March and April when the rhododendrons and other flowers set the forests ablaze with colour. In spring the skies gradually become hazy and there are light rains which may make flights to starting points unpredictable. By May it is hot in Pokhara, the high peaks are rarely visible and humidity mounts until the weather breaks in June with the onset of the monsoon. Trails are thereafter too wet, slippery and leech-ridden for trekking until the rains subside in late September or early October.

The decision on where to go will depend on the time available and your physical condition. Serious trekkers usually plan on spending two to three weeks or more on the trail. A week to five days is probably the minimum to have a fair sampling of trekking life and get your legs in gear. Shorter outings around the Kathmandu Valley, or the three-day "Royal Trek" out of Pokhara which was followed by Prince Charles, afford great mountain views in season and are not to be disdained. Once your route is decided, you'll need two photos for a trekking permit, obtainable by your travel agency or at the Immigration Department in Kathmandu on Dilli Bazaar Road.

You should have a check-up from your doctor at the same time as you get the shots recommended for all visitors to Nepal (see p. 119), and if you are normally desk-bound, try to do as much walking as you can to get in shape before you leave home.

Renting equipment is easy. There are scores of outfitters in Thamel and on Freak Street, often run by Sherpas, offering everything you'll need new or second-hand, that has been sold or given to their crews by earlier trekkers. A deposit may be required for rentals. Hiring a guide and/or porters on your own is risky for the inexperienced. Good advice on whom to hire and what to pay may be obtained from the Trekking Agents Association of Nepal (PO Box 3612; tel. 225875) on Kanti Path opposite the British Council.

Several excellent guidebooks to trekking in Nepal are available and most travel agencies can help you plan a trek or put you in touch with one of Kathmandu's trekking agencies.

On the Trail

Trekking isn't mountain climbing. It's walking, with a lot of up- and downhill stretches. Athletes enjoy the challenge, but you'll also come across groups such as a **87**

women's club from London or gang of kids from an international school in Kathmandu going happily along at their own pace. Anyone can do it. But it is more fun if you are reasonably fit.

A typical trekking day begins around 6 a.m. with a mug of tea outside your tent or lodge as the first rays of sun hit the high peaks above you. Breakfast may be biscuits and porridge, yoghurt or an egg. You'll face up to the latrine problem and then be on your way by 7 a.m. Distances on the trail are measured in hours from place to place, not miles, so it is important to have a

good contour map showing elevations. River valleys run north and south in the mountains while many routes angle east-west, in and out of gorges, involving much ascending and descending on steep trails that are often stone staircases. Two villages that seem close on the map may actually be hours of climbing apart.

You'll marvel at the burdens that porters carry in baskets with headstraps called *dokos*. Everything not made or grown in the villages has to be packed on the backs of wiry barefoot porters who carry loads of 130 pounds (up to 60 kg.) all day long. You'll

Trekking annually draws thousands to walk on the roof of the world.

gets dark, around 6 p.m., and after some chat and a drink by lamplight with villagers and other trekkers, bed will be welcome by 9 p.m.

Along the way you'll watch the hill people working their terraced fields of maize (corn), barley or, in the high country, potatoes. Buffaloes and goats are milked, millet is threshed by pounding the stalks on a threshing floor, grain is ground between two flat stones or pounded in a mortar by a foot-operated rocker-beam. Women endlessly troop to and from distant springs with their water jars, while small children rock babies slung in baskets under the thatched eaves of mud-walled houses. Water-powered grain mills are high-tech. Mini hydro-electric units generating 2 kilowatts are being slowly introduced. One brought electric light for the first time to Thyangboche Monastery in 1988.

notice that porters take short steps on the balls of their feet, knees bent going downhill. Do the same and you'll avoid the common complaint of "Sahib's knee".

On an organized trek the porters will stop for a cooked meal of rice and lentil sauce around 11 a.m. and the day may end around 3 p.m. with setting up tents on a camp ground or finding a village guest house. The sun goes behind the mountains early. Supper will come soon after it

When you stop for a glass of tea or a soft drink, you may be asked to add your name and donation to a list of contributors to the building of a school or bridge, a more official form of the chant of "One pen, please, one rupee please, one sweet" raised by village children. Trekkers are **89**

Debunking the Snowman

Let's face it. The Abominable Snowperson, also known as the Yeti, is probably an illusion. The most abominable thing about the creature is the jokes trekkers have to put up with before and after their trips. True, the Yeti has been reported from 15th-century manuscripts up to the present as a hairy, erect, powerful creature inhabiting the snows of the high Himalayas. Expeditions are sent every few years to find him, her or it. They have described howls in the night, photographed shapeless "footprints" in the snow and brought back tufts of hair usually identified later as coming from goats or bears.

Still the myth lives on, one more among the many legends that come to life in Nepal. And reputable scientists and mountaineers are convinced that there is *something* out there. Tangible proof continues to evade them all.

Chambers of Commerce in California, impressed by Nepal's success with the Yeti, have tried to launch the Sasquatch, or Big-Foot of the Sierras, as a competing cousin. Loch Ness is probably following developments closely.

urged not to give out candy (bad for teeth) or money, and by now the pens are almost in surplus. Gifts to a school teacher for his class are more practical. You'll be asked to put a Bandaid and disinfectant on someone's cut, so have an extra supply handy. Start out with small bills; it may be difficult to change 100-rupee notes. Carry a canteen or a bottle of mineral water (available everywhere) and drink two litres of liquid a day to avoid dehydration.

At times you'll have to give way to caravans of donkeys crowned with red and white yak tail plumes, or yaks themselves in the high country. In the west, sheep are also used as pack animals.

Exciting moments come when you look way up at a towering white cloud and discover that there's a mountain emerging—from *the top*! Or when you inch across a swaying bridge of planks hung from cables over a churning river. Or when there's a booming sound and high on a mountain face an avalanche roars down, seeming in slow motion as it drops thousands of feet. And there's delight in bathing your hot feet in a shady brook or stretching out for a break on a rock platform when porters rest their packs.

The first sight of Everest

close up can never be forgotten. It's the top! But the towering tooth of Ama Dablam above the Thyangboche Monastery, the forked fishtail summit of Macchapuchhare, the solid block of Dhaulagiri, the tent-shaped black rock atop Annapurna II, and the gleaming white of Langtang and Gauri Shankar, as well as other peaks whose names you'll never know, each has its own awesome quality. A mighty power and grandeur emanates from these great mountains, holy to the people who live in their shadow.

Some Popular Treks

Around Everest
(5 days–3 weeks)
The shortest possible trek for a close view of Mount Everest and Sherpa country in Sagarmatha National Park is a five-day dash with round-trip flights between Kathmandu and Lukla. The trail goes up the Dudh Kosi river valley through lovely woodlands with an overnight at Phakding or Jorsale. The next night is at Namche Bazar, where there is a Sherpa market on Saturdays. Return is by the same route, with an added night at Lukla to be on hand for the (often cancelled) early morning flight back.

Add two days for the interesting switchback walk from Namche to the Thyangboche Monastery and back, or ten days for the circuit that goes on to Pheriche for the greatest of all Himalayan views and to the Everest Base Camp area at an exhausting 17,586 feet (5,360 m.) beyond Gorak Shep. Add another week if you go by car or bus from Kathmandu to Jiri and walk to Namche Bazar and back over the Lamjura Pass via Serlo, Junbesi and Khari Khola.

Around Annapurna
(1–3 weeks)
Fly to Pokhara and head for Ghandruk via Dhampus in Gurung country. This avoids high altitudes and circles the spectacular "fishtail" mountain, Macchapuchhare. Continue to Ghorapani above the Kali Gandaki, the world's deepest valley, separating Dhaulagiri and Annapurna I. Return to Pokhara in eight days via Poon Hill and Naudanda. Or add six days round trip and continue from Ghorapani to Tatopani and Jomosom through Thakali villages along the salt-trade trail to Tibet.

Add six days round trip from Ghandruk to Annapurna Sanctuary by way of a fairly rough trail through Chhomro above the Modhi Khola river to Hinko and the Annapurna Base Camp, around 11,500 feet (3,500 m.). The circuit around Annapurna takes 21 days, includes the Jomosom route, a stretch of arid northern Himalaya near Mustang and the 17,790-foot (5,416-m.) Thorung pass.

Around Langtang and Helambu

(6 days–2 weeks)

From Kathmandu, take a car or bus up the Trisuli River valley, an adventure in itself, to Dhunche, entrance to Langtang National Park (there is a small fee to pay, so keep the ticket, it may be requested en route). Making overnight stops at Syabru, Chongong and Langtang Village you reach the Langtang Valley where you pick a campsite near Kyanjin Gompa 12,300 feet (3,749 m.), and its cheese factory set up with Swiss aid. From here you can explore the yak pastures and glaciers beneath snowy Langtang Lirung. Alternative routes lead to the sacred Gosainkund lakes or link up with the popular Helambu circuit for a two-week trek.

The Helambu trail begins at Sundarijal, a cab ride from Kathmandu, and rises through forests to Borlang Bhanjyang, and in one or two days to the Sherpa village of Malemchigaon or to Tharke Gyang and its *gompa* in the Helambu Valley. The return can be via Dhunche or Sundarijal, depending on where you began.

Trekking Tips

Shoes are the most important equipment for trekkers. Some people trek in running shoes, but it is much better to have a light waterproof walking shoe with a firm sole, good tread and ankle support for walking on loose stones. A second pair of tennis shoes can be included for changing at day's end. A light pair of socks covered by a heavier woollen pair makes for comfort going up- and downhill. Be sure to have a roll of moleskin or adhesive plaster to put on your heel or other friction spot *before* blisters form and to make a cushioned hole around any blister. Tight trousers, such as blue jeans, can

Back-packers and yak-packers share spectacular mountain trails.

make for very uncomfortable climbing. Looser trousers, shorts or, for women, a longish loose skirt or harem trousers are the best costume. They are widely sold in Kathmandu and Pokhara. You'll also need extra socks, a change of shirts, and a down jacket.

Take a torch (flashlight), binoculars, sun hat and lotion, dark glasses, water bottle and pocket knife. In your backpack carry a small first-aid kit with disinfectant, gauze pads and adhesive tape, elastic bandage for sprains, insect repellent, tincture of iodine to sterilize water (four drops to a litre), throat lozenges, aspirin and a small pair of scissors, safety pins and a thermometer. Get your doctor to prescribe a treatment for diarrhoea and a wide-spectrum antibiotic. You may be many days from the nearest medical care and will have to doctor yourself and possibly others.

Be aware of the symptoms of Acute Mountain Sickness (AMS) which can suddenly become lethal. The Himalayan Rescue Association (offices in the Kathmandu Guest House in Thamel) advises that headache and breathlessness at any altitude above 6,000 feet (1,800 m.) may be a sign of AMS. Above 10,000 feet (3,000 m.), ascents should not exceed 1,000 feet (300 m.) a day, or a day of rest and acclimatization should intervene before continuing. If symptoms persist, the essential step is to descend as quickly as possible, even if it's night. Results will be dramatic. AMS can hit anyone, even the most fit. Victims are often those macho types who insist on keeping going.

There are no telephones and few places where radio messages may be sent in the mountains or where medical help can be found. Inform yourself where these may be on your route. Helicopters may be chartered from the Royal Nepal Air Force at the princely sum of $2,000 for a few hours, payable in advance. It usually takes about 24 hours, including time for the message to get through, for a rescue to be arranged. Porters can carry an injured person.

Register with your embassy and let them know where you're going and when, and do not trek alone; find a companion through a trekking agency or by posting a notice on one of the many bulletin boards in Thamel.

Do's and Don'ts for Conservation

Nepal is facing an environmental crisis. Cutting down trees that supply 94 per cent of the country's energy has exposed steep mountainsides to erosion, landslides and floods all the way to the Bay of Bengal.

Trekking is a boost for the economy, but it can also add pressure on the environment as forest is felled to meet increasing demands for firewood. Trekkers also litter the landscape with their trash and add to sanitation problems. Scraps of toilet paper found everywhere are known locally as "trekkers' prayer flags".

The King Mahendra Trust for Nature Conservation, headed by a brother of the king, is striving to introduce sound conservation in mountain communities and to educate trekkers. At the headquarters of its Annapurna Conservation Area in the village of Ghandruk on the Annapurna trail, young Gurung activists are promoting the use of fuel-efficient stoves, solar hot-water heating, latrines, tree-planting and locally based forest management. The sale of firewood is prohibited in the Annapurna Sanctuary, which gets 25,000 visitors a year. The King Mahendra Trust has set up a kerosene depot and portable-stove rental at Chhomrong on the way to Annapurna Base Camp.

The Trust has issued a "Minimum Impact Code" for trekkers with the motto "Nepal is Here to Change You, Not for You to Change It." These are some of its golden rules:

- Be self-sufficient in fuel and patronize lodges that use kerosene.
- Campfires and hot showers are a luxury. In view of the fuelwood crisis, use these services sparingly.
- Keep at least 100 feet (30 m.) away from a spring or stream when washing or going to the toilet; bury excreta and toilet paper.
- Burn, bury or pack all rubbish.
- Don't damage, disturb, or remove endangered plants and animals. Stay on trails and camp in designated areas.
- Respect religious shrines and artefacts; respect the customs of Nepali people; dress modestly and avoid outward displays of physical affection.
- Ask permission to photograph people and respect their desire not to be photographed.
- Pay fair prices for goods and services.

What to Do

Sport

Sport is somewhat alien to the hard-working Nepalis. Volley ball is the most popular village game, and martial arts are practised in clubs.

Fishermen can get a good fight out of the mahseer, a giant river carp weighing up to 90 pounds (40 kg.), found in the Karnali, Gandaki and Sun Kosi rivers. Hunting and the importation of firearms is generally discouraged. Current information on which birds and animals may be hunted and how to apply for a licence can be provided by a local travel agent. Big-horned blue sheep are trophies still collectable.

Swimming in the great mountain rivers is dangerous due to strong currents and ice-cold water, but hot springs make for pleasurable bathing.

Jumbo Polo

Ponderous pachyderms pretend to be prancing ponies! Every December the World Elephant Polo Association Championship, a trunk-in-cheek pseudo-sporting event, is staged at Tiger Tops Jungle Lodge. During six days of matches and five nights of replays around the bar, a winner emerges to claim the undisputed world championship. It isn't played anywhere else.

Elephant polo is said to have been invented in the 1930s by the Maharajahs of Jaipur. In 1981 the Tiger Tops management decided to revive it as a competitive event. A field two-thirds the size of a regular polo field was laid out. Patient elephants from the lodge's herd, already trained to carry tourists and do heavy construction work, were given a new assignment of trotting after a little white ball. They seem to enjoy it, especially the balls of rice, molasses and leaves they get as a post-match reward.

Elephant polo uses a standard ball and mallets from 70 to 96 inches (178–250 cm.) long, fitted to the height of the elephant. There are four animals to a side, with the players tied in place by ropes. Each of the two chukkas lasts ten minutes.

Starting with teams recruited at the lodge, the event now attracts squads sponsored by airlines, hotel chains and the National Parks and Wildlife Conservation Department of Nepal. There is even a ladies' event and prizes for the Best Dressed Team—elephants not included.

Polo heavyweights vie for the world title at Tiger Tops.

There are two nine-hole golf courses in Kathmandu, near the airport and at the Gokarna Safari Park just outside the city, where golf clubs can be rented. All the five-star hotels have swimming pools and tennis courts open to visitors for a fee, and there are courts at the National Sports Stadium and Hem's Tennis Centre near the airport.

Mountain bike tours have recently been instituted in Thamel. First-class bikes are available, and tours of several **97** days over the Mahabharat to the Terai and up to Gorkha and Pokhara are guided by experienced bikers. An accompanying van carries camping gear and luggage. Pony trekking outfits operate out of Pokhara.

Entertainment

Singing and dancing at religious festivals and family celebrations are a main source of entertainment in a country that has more yaks than TV sets and a thousand temples for every cinema. In rural Nepal, where there is generally no electricity and everyone, including tourists, is in bed by 9 p.m., as well as in the capital, where the streets are empty by 10 p.m., Western-style entertainment is confined to the hotels and restaurants where foreigners congregate.

In Kathmandu, there are concerts at the Royal Academy, musical comedy in Nepali at the National Theatre and singing and dancing "cultural shows" nightly at the five-star hotels and presented by the Everest Cultural Society in a hall adjoining the Hotel de l'Annapurna. Similar shows are staged by Tharu villagers for guests at the leading Royal Chitwan National Park lodges and in Pokhara. They feature harvest dances, wedding dances, medicine-man rituals and singing with Tibetan or Indian overtones. Nepali drummers are especially talented. In the evenings you can sometimes hear singing at the Seto Machendranath temple off Asan Tole. In villages you may be serenaded by young men with musical instruments. They are *gaine*, Nepali buskers, who expect a tip. They're working, not begging.

The Nepal Casino at the Soaltee Oberoi Hotel is off limits to Nepalis, who are fanatical gamblers at cards, particularly during the *Dasain* and *Tihar* festivals. Rich Indian visitors fill the gaming tables and slot-machine jungles. A free taxi ride back to your hotel is provided at night.

Festivals

With two major religions, a multitude of gods, five calendars and many tribes with their different traditions, it is

Fearsome Bhairav image looks on as Dasain *celebrations animate Kathmandu's Durbar Square.*

98

not surprising that Nepal enjoys a profusion of holidays. Throughout the year the country erupts in colourful festivals that sometimes stretch over weeks. These occasions are usually rooted in a rich compost of fact, legend and ancient seasonal observances. In a land where the round of daily toil can be hard and diversions few, festivals bring a combination of solace, gaiety, confirmation of family ties, plus a bid for good fortune.

Almost all the festivals are moveable feasts, like Easter or Passover, because they relate to the phases of the moon. In addition, some only begin when astrologers declare the auspicious moment. King Birendra's coronation was delayed for more than two years, for example, until the numbers of his age, the year, month and day were all lucky ones. This uncertainty makes it impossible to pinpoint far in advance the dates and times of most festivals. Nevertheless, because there are so many, a visitor can count on some festival taking place during his stay.

Two of the greatest fall during the peak tourist season in October-November. *Dasain* is the most important, comparable to Christmas. It lasts ten days and is followed two weeks later by *Tihar*, the festival of lights. The latter includes the Newari New Year's Day. The official New Year's Day falls on April 14, while the Sherpa holiday, which follows the Chinese calendar, is in February. Nepalis are not confused by these discrepancies. On the contrary, they enthusiastically and impartially share in all festivals, regardless of their origin.

Dasain honours the tiger-riding goddess Durga and her defeat of the buffalo demon Mahisasura, symbolic of good defeating evil. This holiday following the monsoon is a time for renewal, scrubbing the house, wearing new clothes and taking purification baths by starlight at different river locations, followed by temple visits with *puja* offerings of food, coloured powders and flowers. All over the country, children fly kites during *Dasain*, and ferris wheels or swings suspended from four stout bamboo poles are set up on the outskirts of every community. The message carried skywards is "No more rain, please."

On the first day, barley seeds are planted in a special pot in every home. When the barley sprouts on the tenth day, the shoots are worn in the hair or behind the ear. The seventh day is *Phulpati*, the feast of flowers, when a bundle of banana leaves and flowers bound with red ribbon is carried 45 miles (72 km.) to Kathmandu from the old palace of the Shah dynasty at Gorkha. It is borne to the Hanuman Dhoka Durbar in a procession of priests, costumed and masked dancers and bands. Soldiers dressed in the uniforms of the original Gurkhas blaze away with muzzle-loading muskets.

But Durga is also Kali, who thirsts for blood. On the eighth and ninth days of *Dasain*, thousands of chickens, ducks, goats and young buffalo are sacrificed, soaking temples in gore. If you see a taxi with blood on its wheels, don't be alarmed; it should be extra safe. Motorists daub the blood of a sacrificed fowl on their cars for Kali-Durga's protection. Even the aircraft of the Royal Nepal Airlines get this treatment.

You can photograph the head-chopping in the Kot Courtyard off the Durbar Square, where goats and bullocks are sacrificed all morning long for army units. Burly young soldiers are expected to dispatch the animals with a single stroke of the heavy *khora* sword, as the big drum thumps and martial music is played before the massed flags of Nepali regiments. The Kot Courtyard, incidentally, is where the first Rana engineered the massacre of a hundred nobles, clearing the path to power in 1846.

On the tenth day of *Dasain* family members exchange visits and feast. Visits to work supervisors are also obligatory. Government functionaries in their uniform of white leggings, black jacket and cap, go to the palace to receive the *tika* from the king. Thousands of ordinary people also line the streets around the palace, waiting hours to receive the king's blessing.

There is still a celebratory feeling in the air a fortnight later when *Tihar*, also called *Diwali*, arrives. This festival of lights honours Lakshmi, goddess of wealth. The story is that in the dark nights of the autumn new moon, Lakshmi orbits the earth aboard her owl. She will reward with prosperity those houses below that have been made tidy and show lights burning on the doorstep. This is a time for non-stop gambling games, often held on a street corner or **101**

in a temple compound, with all players hoping for Lakshmi's favour. Shops and homes mark a red path on the sidewalk or road into their doors and set out small clay oil lamps to welcome the goddess. Elsewhere, strings of electric lights blaze all night during the five-day festival and groups of youngsters go from house to house singing songs and receiving gifts. All sorts of tinsel garlands, fancy lamps, fireworks and decorations are sold in the street.

During *Tihar*, on successive days, crows, dogs and cows are honoured by giving them treats to eat and garlands to

In Bhadgaon, four days of riotous celebrations precede the Nepali New Year.

the *tika* dot on their forehead and tie a good-luck thread around their left wrist.

Bisket, the official New Year, has a wild celebration in Bhadgaon. Four days before New Year, two groups of men representing two districts of the city have a tug of war over a chariot containing symbols of Kali and Bhairav. The winners keep the chariot in their district and parade it through the streets for the next several days, fuelled by rice liquor. On April 14, a huge pole is erected in a field on the outskirts, decorated with leaves and garlands and two streamers representing snakes.

Snakes? Well, it seems that a princess of bygone years required a new lover every night because each morning her partner was found dead. Until a prince took on the job. After satisfying the princess, he hid himself, sword bared. Two snakes issued from the princess's nostrils, ready to kill. But the prince hacked them up and lived happily ever after with the princess— no questions asked. Her father, the king, ordered the pole with snake streamers to be erected every year in commemoration. Another tug of war takes place on New Year's afternoon, when the pole is

wear. (Cats, by the way, are considered unlucky and are rarely seen in Nepal.) On the fifth day, brothers are honoured by their sisters, who deck them with flowers, place

pulled by opposing teams until it comes crashing down.

Indra Jatra is an important festival, usually falling in early September. During this week-long observance, the Kumari is drawn through the streets of Kathmandu on her chariot and receives the homage of the king. Ritual dances are staged in Durbar Square, which is jam-packed at this time, the steps of the Vishnu temple being reserved for women and children, decked out in their finest. On the last evening, the screen is removed from the face of the White Bhairav mask and beer squirts from his mouth into those of a jostling crowd beneath.

Patan's big blow-out, in late April, is in honour of the Red Machendra, a god sacred to both Buddhists and Hindus and probably of very ancient origin among valley animists. The festival involves dragging a huge chariot across the city and sometimes takes a month before culminating in the display of a jewelled vest, about which, needless to say, another complicated legend exists. Kathmandu's White Machendra gets his chariot ride a month earlier.

Holi, when a kind of may-pole with streamers is put up in Basantapur Chowk next to Kathmandu's old royal palace and crowds throw coloured powders and water bags at each other, comes in March-April, the merriment encouraged by the full moon. *Gaijatra*, the festival of cows and of departed souls, is another light-hearted celebration. Cows are supposed to help enter heaven the souls who hold onto their tails. Boys dressed as cows and clowns dance in the streets, and much booze is consumed, especially at Bhadgaon. During a year after the death of a family member, Nepalis wear white in mourning. White candles also are used at the time of death.

Trekkers who reach the Thyangboche Monastery above Namche Bazar on the full-moon day of November will be priveleged to see the monks' masked dance ceremony, *Mani Rimdu*. A similar dance takes place on the June full moon. Sherpas celebrate Tibetan New Year in February with singing, dancing and the consumption of *chhang*, the local home-brewed rice beer.

A list of festivals and their approximate dates issued annually by the Ministry of Tourism can be obtained from travel agencies.

Calendar of Events

(Because festivals follow different calendars, their dates vary from year to year.)

Jan   *Maghe Sankranti*, marking division between winter and summer. Feasting and river-bathing.

Feb   *Basant Panchami* in honour of Saraswati, Hindu goddess of learning, and first day of spring.
National Democracy Day *(Rashtriya Prajatantra Divas* and *Tribhuvan Jayanti)*. Rallies, processions, pageantry.

Feb-Mar *Maha Shivaratri*, dedicated to Shiva. Hundreds of thousands of devout Hindus go to Pashupatinath to pay their respects. Show by Royal Nepalese Army on Tundikhel parade ground.
Losar, Chinese, Sherpa and Tibetan New Year's Day. Folk dances and songs and lots of potent *chhang* beer.

Mar-Apr *Holi*, festival of colour.
Ghodejatra. Images of gods are carried through the streets in portable chariots. Horse-racing and acrobatics at the Tundikhel parade ground.
Seto (White) *Machendranath*, four-day festival in Kathmandu.
Rato (Red) *Machendranath* in Patan.

Apr   *Bisket*, official Nepali New Year.

May   *Buddha Jayanti* commemorates birth, enlightenment and death of the Buddha. Pilgrimages to major shrines.

July-Aug *Ghanta Karna*, Demon Day to ward off evil spirits.
Naga Panchami, dedicated to worship of the Nagas, the divine serpents. Masked demon dances.

Aug   *Gaijatra*, festival of cows and the departed.

Aug-Sept *Krishna Jayanti*, Krishna's birthday.

Sept   *Indra Jatra*, a week of religious and cultural festivity in Kathmandu.

Sept-Oct *Dasain*, Nepal's major festival lasting ten days.

Oct-Nov *Tihar* and *Lakshmi Puja*, festival of lights.

Dec   *Mani Rimdu*, Buddhist ritual festival of masked dances and blessings given in monasteries of Solu Khumbu.
King Mahendra Memorial and Constitution Day.
King's birthday. Military parades, processions, sporting events.

Shopping

What to Buy

Bring a spare lightweight bag to hold all the gifts you won't be able to resist buying in Nepal. There is something for everyone on your list.

Antiques. Authentic Nepali and Tibetan antiques are increasingly rare, and therefore expensive. They are subject to customs restrictions, so get a certificate from your dealer and, if in doubt, also from the Department of Antiquities to avoid confiscation of your purchase on departure.

Carpets, hand-woven and dyed by the large Tibetan refugee community.

Clothing. Embroidered waistcoats (vests), multicoloured jackets and "harem" trousers in bright materials, knitted sweaters, socks and mittens, Nepali caps known as *topis*.

Kukris. The ornate, curved Gurkha knives.

Jewellery, made with the semi-precious stones found here and in Tibet—turquoise, coral, amethyst, amber, garnets—silver bracelets and amulets.

Masks. Grimacing papier-mâché demon faces.

Shawls. Fine, feather-light cashmere and *pashmina* shawls from the mountains.

Statuettes of Buddhas and Hindu deities cast in bronze or carved in wood.

Tibetan artefacts ranging from cups made from human skulls to long copper horns, silver-lined wooden tea bowls, fur hats and brass "singing bowls" that resonate when their rim is rubbed in a circular motion.

Thangkas. Minutely detailed paintings on Buddhist religious themes or representing the "wheel of life", hand-painted by Newari artists.

Bargaining is expected and even a modest show of resistance will usually bring a small discount quickly. Serious, drawn out bargaining can earn substantial reductions. Competition among sellers is stiff, but it is worth remembering that most of these street merchants are relatively poor, and spending half an hour to extract a few rupees discount is perhaps not the best use of your time.

Nepali handicrafts, from masks to Gurkha kukris and Tibetan bowls, make wonderful gifts.

Where to Shop

The shops in the area around Kathmandu's Durbar Square will give you a good idea of the variety and prices of what's available. In the Basantapur Chowk, the *kukris*, prayer wheels, figurines and grotesque masks are spread on the pavement for your inspection, as well as in the shops in the palace wall facing the temples in the square. Around the walled Taleju temple, *thangka* paintings and papier-mâché masks are displayed in stalls.

The crowded narrow street leading diagonally from Durbar Square to Indra Chowk is the main shopping street for Nepalis as well as tourists. You'll find stalls selling *topis*, the jaunty coloured caps worn by men in the valley, as well as the black ones that are a must for civil servants. All sorts of copper and brass pots are heaped in doorways. Knit sweaters and small rugs hang like laundry overhead. Indra Chowk is the centre for blankets, shawls and sari fabrics. Thamel boasts countless curio shops.

The Durbar Marg leading to the Narayanhiti Palace has, in addition to the street vendors outside hotels, a number of good jewellery shops selling interesting earrings and bangles. Tibetan and Nepali antiques can be found here, as well as at the Mahaguthi shop selling handicrafts from different parts of the country. This is a cooperative venture benefiting rural women. Hand-made paper from the bark of the daphne plant and blockprinted with religious *mandala* designs is sold here.

The best place for carpets with Tibetan or Chinese designs is the Tibetan refugee cooperative in Jawalakhel on the outskirts of Patan. You can see them made here; the prices are fixed and shipment can be arranged on the spot. On the farther side of Patan is the "Industrial Estate", a complex of artisans' workshops and salesrooms where you can watch bronze figurines being cast by the "lost wax" method and then delicately finished by artists. Here, too, are the woodcarvers who still preserve the skills that created the temple decorations and ornamental windows of the valley.

Bhadgaon is the place for *thangkas* and other paintings. Thimi village is where many of the masks are made and where interesting pottery, including flower pots in the shape of elephants, is sold.

Eating Out

Nepal's national dish is *dhal baat*, lentils and rice, jazzed up with hot chilli pepper and some greens. It's cheap and nutritious, but haute cuisine it's not. In Sherpa country, potatoes are the staple, cooked a variety of ways, but most elaborately as *gurr*, spiced potato pancakes grilled and eaten with cheese. Beef, of course, is taboo in a Hindu country.

The most tasty local specialities are borrowed from Tibetan or Indian cooking. From Tibet come *miso*, noodle soup, and fried or steamed *momos*, dumplings filled ravioli-style with minced pork, garlic and cabbage. The Tibetan *gyakok*, served in a "chimney pot" over a flame, contains meat, vegetables and

Tibetan "chimney pot"—meat and vegetables cooked in broth—makes a festive repast.

chicken in a rich broth. It usually has to be ordered several hours in advance. Indian influence can be seen in the variety of vegetarian or mutton or chicken curries and *tandoori* dishes.

Tea is the favoured drink, brewed with milk, sugar and sometimes spices, and with yak butter in the high mountains. Local beer is good, wine prohibitively expensive. Fresh limeade and *lassi*, yoghurt thinned with iced water, make refreshing drinks.

Where to Eat
A good place to sample Nepali cuisine is the Sun Kosi on Durbar Marg, but there are quite a few good restaurants in Kathmandu serving international specialities in the all-important hygienic settings. These include Chinese, Japanese, Korean, French, Italian, Austrian and American establishments. Some feature entertainment, such as Rajasthani singing in the Hotel de l'Annapurna's Ghar e Kebab restaurant that accompanies authentic *mughlai* cuisine, and the musical evenings at K.C.'s are popular with trekkers in Thamel. The candle-lit crowded bistros of Thamel are lively and atmospheric.

The hotels are good bets. The Yak and Yeti serves an elegant meal in the chandelier-hung dining hall of a former palace, with a stage show of Nepali dancers. Veteran travellers who remember when Boris's Yak and Yeti restaurant in the old Royal Hotel was *the* place to meet and eat will be happy to find it recreated intact in the Hotel Yak and Yeti's Chimney Restaurant. The Soaltee Oberoi, offering dinner dancing, and the Everest Sheraton, with a rooftop view over the mountains and city, have restaurants serving both continental and oriental menus.

In Thamel, breakfast spots cater to people staying in guest houses, which do not usually have kitchens. A number of inexpensive eateries advertise that they boil and filter water and sterilize vegetables.

Trekking cooks have been taught these rules and some of the lodges on the trekking trail are getting the message, too. Washing your hands frequently and avoiding unbottled water, ice and uncooked greens will help stave off the dread "Kathmandu Quickstep" tummy troubles. No matter how tempting it looks, it is best to abstain from the fare available from street stalls.

BLUEPRINT for a Perfect Trip

How to Get There

Because of the complexity and variability of the many fares, you should ask the advice of an informed travel agent well before your departure.

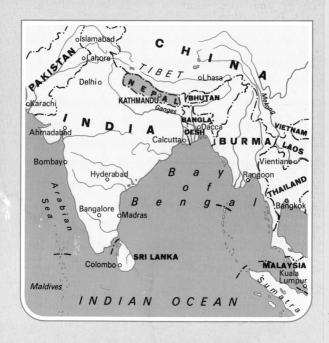

BY AIR

Scheduled flights. Kathmandu's Tribhuvan International Airport receives more than 90 per cent of non-Indian visitors to Nepal. At present the only direct flights from Europe are from Frankfurt, flying time between 11 and 12 hours. Flights from elsewhere in Europe and from North American cities require a change at Frankfurt or, for the most part, Delhi, which has the largest number of connections to Kathmandu.

Charter flights and package tours. Royal Nepal Airlines (RNAC) extends charter flights to all domestic airports and from time to time on international routes.

Overland. The main crossing point for buses to and from India by road is Bhairawa in Nepal and Nautanwa on the Indian side. Indian trains are good, and a bus-train combination from Delhi, Varanasi (Benares) or Patna is possible. Travel within Nepal would be by bus, a generally crowded and uncomfortable service. From China (Tibet) the road crossing is at Kodari. Sections of the highway are sometimes closed by landslides; in such cases travellers may have to walk part of the distance to be met on the other side of the impasse by another vehicle.

When to Go

October and November are sunny and pleasantly warm. Facilities for tourism are at their most crowded at this season. December through February are marked by wonderfully clear skies but are chilly, especially for trekkers. March and April find the rhododendrons at their peak in the mountains and are the second most popular months, after autumn. May is hot and humid at low altitudes. The monsoon rains begin in June and continue through September.

The following chart gives average maximum and minimum daily temperatures for Kathmandu.

		J	F	M	A	M	J	J	A	S	O	N	D
Maximum	°F	63	66	75	81	82	82	82	82	81	77	72	66
	°C	17	19	24	27	28	28	28	28	27	25	22	19
Minimum	°F	36	37	44	52	61	66	68	68	64	55	44	37
	°C	2	3	7	11	16	19	20	20	18	13	7	3

* Minimum temperatures are measured just before sunrise, maximum temperatures in the afternoon.

Planning Your Budget

To give you an idea of what to expect, here are a few average prices in Nepali rupees (Rs). Certain expenses, airline tickets, hotels, car hire are supposed to be paid in hard currency and are therefore listed below in U.S. dollars ($). All prices, however, can only be approximate, as inflation takes its toll.

Airport. Airport bus to Kathmandu Rs 15; taxi to city centre Rs 30–50. Departure tax Rs 200 for international flights, Rs 30 for domestic flights. Porter Rs 5 per bag.

Airfares. Mountain flight $75; return (round-trip) to Pokhara $100, to Lukla $130.

Baby-sitting. Rs 50 per hour.

Bicycle Hire. Per day Rs 15–20.

Car Hire. Full day within Kathmandu Valley, with driver, about $20–40; to Pokhara $55; to the Royal Chitwan National Park $70.

Cigarettes. Imported brands Rs 35–45 per packet of 20; local brands Rs 3–13.

Entertainment. Folklore dance and song show Rs 50. Cinema Rs 1–15.

Guides. Rs 200 per day, plus room and board on overnight trips.

Hairdressers. In hotels, *Woman's* shampoo and set Rs 120; *man's* cut Rs 40. Prices in town establishments considerably less.

Hotels (double room with bath per night). *Luxury* $100, plus 15% tax; *moderate* $70, plus 14% tax; *guest houses* $10–30, plus 10% tax.

Meals and drinks. Hotel breakfast Rs 150–200, lunch Rs 200–350, dinner Rs 200–400. Lunch/dinner in restaurant Rs 50–250. Soft drinks Rs 5 (in hotels Rs 15), beer Rs 30 (in hotels Rs 50), pot of tea Rs 10–35. Glass of tea on trek Rs 1–2.

Taxis and tempos. Average city ride in metered taxi Rs 10, without meter Rs 20; *tempo* with meter, average ride Rs 7, without meter Rs 2–3. Rickshaw, average ride Rs 10.

Tours. Half day within Kathmandu and its valley in private car with guide $25; in bus $3. Half day outside Kathmandu Valley in private car with guide, approximately $30–50 (depending on distance).

An A-Z Summary of Practical Information and Facts

A **ACCOMMODATION**. Kathmandu offers the full range, from luxury (five-star) hotels to dozens of simple but clean guest houses. The government's star rating system is based on size of rooms and amenities provided, such as swimming pool, travel agency, hairdresser, shops and international cuisine. Nevertheless, hotels with only two or three stars that lack some luxury services may have especially attractive gardens, antique furnishings, or even be housed in a former palace.

Outside the capital, first-class accommodation is found in Pokhara, the starting point for many treks. The top jungle camps in the Royal Chitwan National Park combine roughing it with solid comfort. Trekkers can choose among abundant rudimentary guest houses in villages along popular routes.

During the busiest months, October–December and March–May, advance booking is advisable. At other times reductions of 30 per cent or more may be negotiated. Travellers arriving at Kathmandu airport without a hotel reservation should consult the Nepal Hotel Association desk there for advice and bookings.

AIRPORT. Tribhuvan International Airport is a crowded facility 15 minutes' drive east of Kathmandu. The first thing you see on disembarking is a duty-free shop for arriving passengers. The entry formalities don't take long. An airport bus geared to budget-conscious tourists takes passengers to New Road, Durbar Marg and the Provident Trust building on the edge of Thamel. Taxis are also available.

When leaving Nepal, be at the airport at least two hours before departure time, as flights are crowded and much standing in line ensues.

B **BABY-SITTERS.** English-speaking baby-sitters can be provided by the bigger hotels at a few hours' notice.

BICYCLE HIRE. Sturdy bikes are widely available for rent, especially in Kathmandu's Thamel district. Cycling is one of the best ways to see the Kathmandu Valley, which is mostly flat, but in town you'll need steady nerves to navigate through crowds of people, cows, rickshaws and honking traffic. Make sure the bell works. For a few rupees, a boy will watch your parked bike while you are shopping or exploring. Mountain-bike touring is offered by an American-run agency in Thamel.

CAR HIRE. Cars can only be hired with a driver. International and local rental agencies have desks in travel agencies and in the main hotels. Rates (payable in hard currency) vary considerably; it is definitely worthwhile shopping around.

CALENDAR. Nepal entered the 21st century in 1943, according to the official calendar used for government purposes, in newspapers and by most Nepalis in their everyday lives. Legend relates that the benevolent king Bikramaditya paid off all the debts of his subjects on April 14, 57 B.C. and started the new calendar from scratch. The Western Gregorian calendar is in everyday use by hotels, agencies and airlines, so travellers need not be confused. However, three other calendars are also used in parts of Nepal.

CIGARETTES, CIGARS AND TOBACCO. For Nepalis, the cheapest and therefore most widely smoked variety of cigarette is the *bidi*, various mixed herbs (none harmful) rolled in a thin cone of brown paper. There are other higher-quality local brands, and foreign brands are also available (but are more expensive). As in many poor countries, cigarettes can be bought singly.

CLOTHING. Unless you are expecting to attend a diplomatic or official function you'll never need a necktie nor a long dress in Kathmandu. Even visitors who don't intend to trek farther than the taxi stand can be seen in safari styles. Sweaters and jackets are enough to cope with autumn and winter evenings in town. During the rainy months, June–September, umbrellas are better than raincoats which are too hot for comfort. In the mild spring and autumn, cool leisure wear is suitable at all hours.

COMMUNICATIONS

Post office. The General Post Office on Kanti Path opens 10 a.m. to 5 p.m. (4 p.m. in winter), Sunday to Friday and closes on Saturdays. **115**

C Staff also sell stamps outside its doors from 8.30 to 10.30 a.m. and from 2.30 to 6 p.m. A special Foreign Post Office is located next door, which handles parcels to be sent abroad. Contents will be examined by a Customs Officer and the parcel will then be stitched in cloth and sealed with wax on the spot for a small charge. The FPO counter is open from 10 a.m. (but staff are rarely there before 10.30) to 2.30 p.m., Sunday through Friday, closing at 12.30 p.m. on Fridays. Airmail letters to Europe and America can easily take two weeks.

Telephone. Nepal is linked by satellite to the phone systems of the world and there is direct dialling to 34 countries.

Some useful numbers:	Enquiries	197
	Internal Trunk Calls	180
	International Operator	186
	Calls to India	187

Telegrams and telex. First-class hotels have telex facilities, as do some travel agencies. The Central Telegraph Office, Tripureshwar, deals with telephone calls, cables and telexes.

CUSTOMS AND ENTRY REGULATIONS

Visas. Visas valid for 30 days may be obtained without delay from Royal Nepalese Embassies or Consulates. Indian citizens do not need a visa. Two photos are required and a fee is payable. Travellers without visas can get one good for seven or 15 days at the airport on arrival. These can be extended for up to a month at a time (unless you get a trekking permit for a longer period than a month at the same time as the visa extension) for a maximum of three months at the Central Immigration Office, Maiti Devi, Kathmandu. Extension applications must be accompanied by receipts showing that the equivalent of $10 has been exchanged for each day of extension requested.

Currency restrictions. There is no limit to the amount of foreign currency you may bring into Nepal but you must fill out a currency declaration form on entry that will be retained at the airport. This will not be checked on departure unless you wish to exchange Nepalese money for hard currency. Then you will have to produce receipts for exchange transactions and will be allowed to convert up to 10 per cent of the amount on record. To have enough documentation for this purpose, always ask for receipts when you change money. Importing or exporting Nepalese or Indian currency is prohibited to non-Indians.

The following chart shows what main items you can take into Nepal
duty-free, and, on returning, into your home country.

Into	Cigarettes		Cigars		Tobacco	Spirits		Wine
Nepal	200	or	500 gr.	or	1 l.	1 l.	or	
Australia	200	or	250 g.	or	250 g.	1 l.	or	1 l.
Canada	200	and	50	and	900 g.	1.1 l.	and	1.1 l.
Eire	200	or	50	and	250 g.	1 l.	or	1 l.
Japan	200	or	50	and	250 g.	3 l.	or	3 l.
N. Zealand	200	or	50	and	½ lb.	1 qt.	or	1 qt.
U.K.	200	or	50	and	250 g.	1 l.	or	2 l.
U.S.A.	200	and	100	or	*	1 l.	and	1 l.
*a reasonable quantity								

ELECTRIC CURRENT. Throughout Nepal the current is 220 volts
A.C. and 50 cycles. First-class hotels have outlets for electric shavers
and hair dryers that convert 110 volts and adapt to Western plugs. A
three round pin plug is standard in Nepal.

EMBASSIES AND CONSULATES. Following is a list of the foreign
missions in Kathmandu.

Australia	Bhat Bhateni; tel. 411578 or 411304
India	Embassy, Lainchur; tel. 410900
U.K.	Embassy, Lainchur; tel. 410583 or 411789
U.S.A.	Embassy, Panipokhari; tel. 411179 or 411601. Consular section, Maharajgunj; tel. 413602

Nepalese missions abroad:

Australia	Consulate, Suite 601, 126 Wellington Parade, East Melbourne, Victoria; tel. 419 8783
	House of Kathmandu, 66 High Street, Toowong 4066, Brisbane; tel. (07) 371 4228
	24th floor, Airways House, 195 Adelaide Terrace, Perth; tel. 221 1207
Canada	Consulate, 310 Dupont Street, Toronto, Ontario; tel. (416) 968 7252

E **India**　　　　Embassy, 1 Barakhamba Rd., New Delhi 110001; tel. 332 99 69
Consulate, 19, Woodlands, Sterndale Road, Calcutta; tel. 45 02 24

Japan　　　　Embassy, 14–9, Todoroki, 7-chome, Setagaya-ku, Tokyo; tel. 705 5558/9

U.K.　　　　Embassy, 12A Kensington Palace Gardens, London W8 4QU; tel. (01) 229 1594

U.S.A.　　　Embassy, 2131 Leroy Place N.W., Washington D.C. 20008, tel. (202) 667 4550
Permanent Mission to U.N., 820 Second Avenue, Suite 1200, New York, N.Y. 10017; tel. 370 4188/9
Consulate, 1500 Lake Shore Drive, Chicago, Illinois
Consulate, 909, Montgomery Street, Suite 400, San Francisco, California 94111; tel. (415) 434 1111

EMERGENCIES. In an emergency you can ring the following numbers:　Police　　　216999
　　　　　　　　Ambulance　215094
　　　　　　　　Fire　　　　211177

G **GETTING AROUND**

Taxis. Registered taxis with meters are recognizable by their black licence plates with white numbers; private taxis have no meters and sport red and white number plates, as do all other private cars. Private taxis cost more than the metered variety and the fare should be agreed upon before departure. Many drivers of registered taxis refuse to turn the meter on or insist it is "broken".

Tempos and rickshaws. The three-wheeled *tempo* motorbike rickshaws cost about half as much as taxis, if they are willing to use the meter. Bicycle rickshaws are not metered and require bargaining. They usually end up at more than the motorized variety but are more fun.

Buses. This is the cheapest way to travel in Nepal. Buses to the nearby cities of Patan and Bhadgaon are more colourful than comfortable when crammed with commuting workers. Those that serve the routes to Chitwan and Pokhara range from the crowded and uncomfortable regular and overnight buses to special non-stop tourist coaches. Buses going beyond the Kathmandu Valley leave from points near the General Post Office or the main bus station opposite the Tundikhel parade ground. Your hotel will advise you on where to catch the bus that you want.

118

Roads. The road system in Nepal links the capital with Pokhara and the Chinese border entry point for Tibet and connects with Indian border crossings along the main east-west highway running most of the length of the country through the Terai lowlands. There are over 4,000 miles (6,000 km.) of roads, nearly half of them all-weather roads in various states of repair, but the steep terrain, hairpin curves and the presence of wandering animals and slow-moving or broken-down buses and trucks make road travel a great spectacle—in slow motion.

Internal flights. Royal Nepal Airlines (RNAC), the national flag carrier, operates scheduled flights to airports around the country, many of them grass strips in mountain areas otherwise only reachable by days of trekking. These strips are surrounded by high peaks and are cloud-covered much of the time. This means that flights are often cancelled or greatly delayed, for pilots can only fly in clear weather. In the most popular trekking seasons there are simply not enough planes to meet the demand for tickets to places such as Lukla and Pokhara, jumping-off points for Everest and Annapurna treks. Over-booking is compounded by backlogs created when flights are cancelled. In such cases the hapless traveller moves to the bottom of the waiting list for the next available seat. It is therefore most important to have return bookings confirmed before leaving Kathmandu, reconfirmed on arrival and to allow for the possibility of being stuck in the mountains for four or five days longer than planned.

GUIDES AND TOURS. There are organized bus tours around Kathmandu and to Patan and Bhadgaon. These offer a good way to cover the ground in a short time. All are of course conducted by experienced guides able to speak foreign languages. Such guides can also be retained privately through travel agencies in Kathmandu.

HEALTH AND MEDICAL CARE. Hygiene and sanitation have steadily improved in Kathmandu in recent years. Nevertheless, tummy troubles such as the notorious "Kathmandu Quickstep" and more serious ailments are common throughout the country and can spoil your trip if you don't take sensible precautions. Before leaving home consult your doctor on recommended vaccinations and what to bring in a personal medical kit. Shots or boosters for cholera, polio and typhoid-tetanus are standard, though vaccination certificates are rarely checked on entry. A meningitis vaccination is recommended (but difficult to arrange in Western countries) and gamma globulin for hepatitis resistance are often prescribed. Malaria tablets should be

H   taken by anyone intending to visit the jungle areas for extensive periods; malaria was nearly eradicated 20 years ago, but has made a slight comeback since.

Many prescription drugs can be bought over the counter in Nepal, but to be safe bring along sufficient amounts of special medication you may require and extra prescription glasses. Medical care, scarce outside the capital and the few large towns, is virtually non-existent in vast stretches of trekking country. In Kathmandu, some embassies have a staff doctor or will recommend a reputable physician or dentist in an emergency.

L   **LANGUAGE.** The official language, Nepali, is akin to Hindi and uses the same script, Devanagari. In addition, there are 33 officially recognized languages (although anthropologists have counted up to 100), plus innumerable dialects. Nepal's languages are mainly Indo-Aryan or Tibeto-Burman tongues. Many shopkeepers and school children in the Kathmandu Valley speak some English.

LAUNDRY AND DRY-CLEANING. All hotels and guest houses can arrange to have laundry done and returned the same day at no extra charge. Dry-cleaning is available in the better hotels, as well as in town.

M   **MAPS.** Maps of Kathmandu and its valley prepared by the government Survey Department are probably the best and are available in book stores. Streets in the capital are generally not marked, so maps are helpful. Orient yourself by a prominent landmark, such as the Tundikhel parade ground in Kathmandu. For trekking, the "Schneider" maps of the Munich Technical University, available in book stores, are good. Trekking agencies usually provide special maps covering specific routes. It is important to have contour maps showing elevations; on a trek it is not the kilometres to your goal that count, but rather the time each stage will take, greatly influenced by the height of the ascents and descents en route.

The maps in this guide were prepared by Falk-Verlag, Hamburg.

MEETING PEOPLE. Nepalis are a genuinely hospitable people. A smile and mastery of at least some phrases of Nepali will always earn a warm response. On the trail you'll have many opportunities to see how people live and to converse with school teachers and others who speak English, perhaps a retired Gurkha soldier. But in town don't be **120** surprised if a friendly conversation that began with the question

"Where are you from?" turns into a sales pitch. Don't be offended if some Nepalis seem to avoid your invitation to share a meal. This would be forbidden to a Brahmin, for example.

MONEY MATTERS

Currency. The unit of currency in Nepal is the Nepali rupee (abbreviated Rs), divided into 100 paisa.

Banknotes: 1, 2, 5, 10, 20, 50, 100, 500 and 1,000 rupees
Coins: 1 and 2 paisa (rare), 5, 10, 25, 50 paisa and 1 rupee

Banks and currency exchange. Nepali rupees can be bought at the airport on arrival, a special foreign exchange counter of Nepal Bank Limited in New Road (open 7.30 a.m. to 6 p.m.) and many hotels and travel agencies authorized by the Nepal Rastra Bank (State Bank of Nepal). Main offices of other banks open 10 a.m. to 2 p.m., Sunday to Thursday, and 10 a.m. to noon on Fridays. Take your passport when changing money and keep the receipts; you will need to show them if you wish to change Nepali rupees back into hard currency on departure. You may be accosted in the street with offers to change money at blackmarket rates. Shopkeepers may also propose payment in hard currency at premium rates. It isn't worth the risk. Technically, all hotel bills must be paid in hard currency, but it amounts to the same thing if you pay in rupees exchanged officially. Nevertheless, you may be asked to produce hard currency for these expenses.

Credit cards and traveller's cheques. Major credit cards are accepted by the better hotels, airline offices, travel agencies, trekking agents, and by an increasing number of shops.

MOUNTAIN FLIGHT. Royal Nepal Airlines operates a one-hour daily flight from Kathmandu that follows the Himalayas eastwards and comes close to Mount Everest. If the mountains are covered by bad weather, the flights are cancelled. They are suspended during the monsoon season.

NEWSPAPERS AND MAGAZINES. Kathmandu's largest-circulation English-language daily newspaper *The Rising Nepal*, a government-owned publication, contains a fair section of foreign news along with accounts of royal doings, bicycle thefts and cricket results. *The International Herald Tribune* and international editions of newspapers and magazines are also widely available, although sometimes arrive a day or two late.

O   **OPENING HOURS.** Public offices are open from 10 a.m. to 5 p.m., Sunday to Thursday, 10 a.m. to 3 p.m. on Fridays, and are closed on Saturdays. Between mid-November and mid-February, offices close one hour earlier.

Shops, travel agencies and airlines don't usually open before 9 a.m. but stay open until 7 p.m. or later. Foreign diplomatic offices and international agencies are closed Saturday and Sunday.

P   **PHOTOGRAPHY.** Amateur and professional photographers go wild in Nepal. Bring plenty of film, but when you run out be careful to look at the expiration date of the film that you buy; old film from India is marketed here. Most kinds are available and colour prints can be delivered in an hour at centrally located automatic processing shops. Slides are best developed when you return home. A polaroid or UV filter will be useful for mountain photography. Except in the clear winter months, clouds often cover the peaks after 10 a.m. A telephoto zoom lens is very useful in both mountains and the jungle.

POLICE. The main police station is situated at Hanuman Dokha, Durbar Square. Policemen and women wear khaki uniforms with dark red berets, except for traffic police, who sport dark blue uniforms with white caps, belts and puttees. There are police posted in booths at main points of tourist concentration, such as the central crossroads of Thamel and Durbar Square in Kathmandu. Police constables don't speak English, but their officers usually do.

Outside the Kathmandu Valley there are zonal and district police stations.

PUBLIC HOLIDAYS (see also p. 105). There are more than 30 days of official holidays during which some or all government offices will be closed. Travel agencies, airline offices and most shops will be open at least part of the time during prolonged holidays, such as the ten-day *Dasain* festival that falls in September or October.

The dates of important festivals are usually linked to phases of the moon. The timing of these moveable feasts is made harder to establish by the reliance on astrologers, who often wait until the last minute to declare a date auspicious. The Ministry of Tourism issues an approximate calendar of festivals a year in advance.

R   **RADIO AND TV.** TV is at present largely confined to the Kathmandu Valley. Nepal Television broadcasts for 3½ hours daily, 5½ hours on Saturday. There is one news broadcast in English daily on the television, which can be seen in the lobbies of some hotels. Two news bulletins are broadcast every day on the radio in English. Much of the rest of the air time is devoted to popular songs in the Indian style.

RELIGIOUS SERVICES. Inter-denominational Protestant services in English are held in Kathmandu on Sunday at the Lincoln School, Kalimati. Roman Catholic services in English are held on Saturday evening at the Hotel de l'Annapurna, Durbar Marg, and Sunday, morning and evening, at St. Xavier's Church in Jawalakhel, Patan.

TABOOS AND CUSTOMS. The traditional greeting is "Namaste", meaning "I salute the divine in you.", with hands held in a praying position close to the chest. Don't place your hand on anyone's head. Offer a gift with both hands and in any case, never with the left hand only. Walk around temples and shrines clockwise and remove shoes where indicated on entering a temple compound or a private house. It is considered improper for women to expose flesh above the knee; however, so many foreigners unaware of this wear shorts that the custom may be overwhelmed before long.

TIME DIFFERENCE. Nepal is 15 minutes ahead of Indian Standard Time and five hours 45 minutes ahead of Greenwich Mean Time (GMT). The following chart shows winter times in selected cities. In summer, when U.S. and European clocks advance one hour, Nepal stays the same.

New York	London	**Nepal**	Sydney
1.15 a.m.	6.15 a.m.	**noon**	4.15 p.m.

TIPPING. Service is not usually included on hotel and restaurant bills. Ten per cent is an acceptable tip for waiters in establishments patronized by Westerners. Elsewhere a tip may be welcome but is not necessary. The official charge for porters carrying bags at the airport is Rs 1 per bag, but even Nepalis agree this is too low; Rs 3–5 per bag is fairer. Taxis do not demand a tip, but will appreciate a few rupees. The driver of a hired car will expect Rs 30–50 at the end of a day. Keep a good supply of 1- and 2-rupee notes for tipping purposes.

TOILETS. Outside the better hotels and tourist facilities, Western travellers will find toilets to be off-putting. The hole-in-the-floor-with-footrests variety dominates and there will rarely be any toilet paper.

T Always carry your own. Necessity will overcome much squeamishness. On the trail, some trekking agencies put up toilet tents. More likely you will follow local custom and use the bushes. The carelessness of many trekkers in covering the landscape with bits of toilet paper has been deplored by Sir Edmund Hillary, among others. A good trekker digs a small hole and then covers his tracks.

TOURIST INFORMATION OFFICES. The government tourist information offices can answer questions on hotels, sightseeing, fares and rates and supply maps and brochures, but they do not handle hotel or air bookings. The government produces good brochures, available abroad at Royal Nepalese Embassies and consulates. Travel agencies can provide these, too, along with other material relevant to your itinerary.

The main Tourist Information Centre in Kathmandu is at Ganga Path, Basantapur; tel. 215818. There are also tourist information desks at Tribhuvan International Airport, at Birganj, Pokhara airport and Bhairawa.

W **WATER.** Even long-time foreign residents of Nepal boil and filter their water. This is a precaution that must be taken very seriously, for, in addition to simple but annoying diarrhoea, hepatitis, amoebic dysentry, typhoid fever and cholera are all real health risks. The better hotels provide boiled and filtered water in jugs in the rooms. Bottled mineral water is widely available, even in mountain villages, as are tea, soft drinks and beer, with prices rising along with the distance the bottles have been carried.

WEIGHTS AND MEASURES. Nepal uses the metric system and measures temperature in centigrade.

Length

cm	0	5	10	15	20	25	30
inches	0	2	4	6	8	10	12
metres	0		1 m				2 m
ft./yd.	0	1 ft.		1 yd.			2 yd.

Weight

grams	0	100	200	300	400	500	600	700	800	900	1 kg
ounces	0	4	8	12	1 lb.	20	24	28	2 lb.		

SOME USEFUL EXPRESSIONS

hello/goodbye	**namaste**
How are you?	**Sanchai chha?**
yes/no/OK	**ju/hoina/hajur**
please/thank you	**kripaya/dhanyabad**
excuse me	**maap-hi garnus**
now/after	**ahile/pachi**
today/tomorrow	**aaja/bholi**
where/when/how	**kahaa/kaile/kasri**
How many hours to..?	**... kati ghan taa?**
left/right	**bayaa/daya**
near/far	**najik/tadhaa**
Is this the road going to ..?	**... jaane baato ho?**
uphill/downhill	**ukhalo/orallo**
good/bad/tasty	**ramro/naramro/mit-ho chha**
big/little/enough	**thulo/saanao/pugyo**
hot/cold	**taato/chiso**
clean/dirty	**saphaa/phohar**
quickly/slowly	**chhito/bistaarai**
Give me only a little.	**Ali ali dinos.**
How much for this?	**Yasko kati?**
expensive	**mahago**
food/water	**khaanaa/paani**
tea/coffee	**chiyaa/kaphi**
Where is the toilet?	**Chharpi kahaa chha?**
What time is it?	**Kati bajyo?**
I don't understand.	**Maile bujhina.**
Please say it again.	**Pheri bhannos.**
What is your name?	**Tapaaiko naam ke ho?**
I am sick.	**Birami chhu.**
I have a headache.	**Malaai/mero taauko dukhyo.**
My legs hurt.	**Mero khuttaa dukhyo.**
I have altitude sickness.	**Lekh laagyo.**

Numbers

one	**ek**	six	**chha**
two	**dui**	seven	**saat**
three	**tin**	eight	**aath**
four	**chaar**	nine	**nau**
five	**paanch**	ten	**das**

Index

An asterisk (*) next to a page number indicates a map reference. Where there is more than one set of page references, the one in bold type refers to the main entry.